In Search
Of Pearls

Sharon Estrada

In Search Of Pearls

Sharon Estrada

ISBN 1-55630-501-X

PUBLISHED BY:
BRENTWOOD CHRISTIAN PRESS
4000 BEALLWOOD AVENUE
COLUMBUS, GEORGIA 31904

Dedication

To JOHN ESTRADA, who let me be me. Although not understanding my many moods and dysfunctions until our 30th year of marriage, he stood by me. After he saw my pain, he encouraged me to do what God had called me to do. His constant prayers and support are what keep me going. He is my best earthly friend, not jealous of the time I spend with this mission and my new Partner, the Healer. Thanks Honey, for walking beside me!

This book is also dedicated to our daughters, Teresa and Angela. Thank you both for making life enjoyable again and for your understanding of a broken Mom.

IN SEARCH OF PEARLS is especially dedicated to the memory of our only son, Matthew Irving Estrada, 1960-1979, who, even in death, continues to inspire me.

Acknowledgements

Special thanks to:

Sandy Powell and Mabel Shankel who gave me the opportunity to speak out in a safe place in 1989.

Sara Miller who encouraged me to write this book.

Jim Thurmon, Doug Hilliard, Clinton Shankel, Helen Boskind, Mauneza Lyons, Richard Hallock, and "the cousins" for their support and encouragement.

Judy Carpenter who spent hours typing, re-typing and getting the manuscript ready for publication.

Shari, Rosemary, Patricia, and all the others who gave unselfishly of their time to do volunteer work for the ministry.

Judy, Dean, Marlys and Patricia who took time away from home and family duties to travel with me.

Dr. Kay Kuzma who praised the final draft and continued to inspire and encourage me.

Contents

Preface

Reading and research have only proven to confirm or affirm my own ways of coping and dealing with recovery. In II Chronicles 18:17, New International Version, it seems that Ahab didn't like the message from the prophet. "Didn't I tell you, he never prophesies anything good about me, but only bad?" And in verse 23, Zedekiah slapped Micaiah in the face." He didn't like what the prophet told him either.

IN SEARCH OF PEARLS will open the eyes of many Christians as to what is happening to our children. Some may not believe, others will be shocked, more will be thankful that someone was at last brave enough to say these things out loud. Still others will want to "slap the prophet."

This book has taken years to prepare. My files bulge with stories of adults, at last speaking about their pain, after years of silence and with stories of children dealing with present issues. Childhood sexual abuse is a very real problem and "slapping the prophet" will not change the reality. Now is the time to embrace the reality and the victims of this malignant abuse.

There is something we should say about statistics. Given the variables such as place or institutions, understanding of the subject, time in history, and the honesty of participants, numbers can range greatly. I will use statistics from various surveys, some of my own, and from my own experience, some "gut feelings." Regardless of all the surveys done or attempted, we know the percentages are high and perhaps even greater than we ever dreamed. Outcomes are colored to the greatest extent by understanding of information requested and the total honesty of participants.

Male victims are the most likely to be less than honest because most were taught as children, "Big boys don't cry. Stand up and take it like a man. Don't be a sissy."

Society as a whole has never given boys permission to cry or express their feelings of pain and disappointment. Male victims of abuse think they are "less than a man" if they admit to having been "taken advantage of."

The misunderstanding of what sexual abuse really is, also distorts survey percentages. To some, oral sex and anal intercourse are sexual abuse, while fondling, french-kissing, exposure and gestures are not. We will attempt to answer these and other questions in understandable language. When you have finished reading this book, I hope you can see the urgency of getting legislation passed to educate children, validate victims, and hold abusers accountable. The Lord is with us in this quest.

II Chronicles 15:1-2 (Today's English Version) says "The Lord is with you as long as you are with Him. If you look for Him, he will let you find Him, but if you turn away, He will abandon you."

If we continue to deny these things are happening among us, we are doing less than is expected of us. This book is not intended to entertain but to inform you.

"Speak up for the people who cannot speak for themselves. Protect the rights of all who are helpless." Proverbs 31:8 (New International Version)

1

Innocence Violated

(One Small Pearl)

She was a very young girl, just a child. It happened when she was only seven years old, six weeks before her eighth birthday. One evening, her ten and a half year old brother had tricked her, saying that the family cat had babies in the farm building. Loving kittens as she did, she lost no time in getting there. If she waited longer, it would be dark and she might not be able to see the little furry bundles until morning and her curiosity could not wait that long. Off she went, not questioning the truth of the matter. Instead, when she arrived at the farm building, she found herself surrounded by teenage boys from her neighborhood, and the cat was nowhere in sight.

She knew all of the boys. It was a small community and the kids rode the same school bus. The bus stop was at the small country store in the rural community. The younger children were let out at the elementary school at the bottom of the hill just three and a half miles away, while the older kids were transported into town to junior high and high school. Time on the bus gave the kids plenty of time to get acquainted.

Not expecting to see the boys in the barn, she was caught off guard at the scene before her. Something was wrong. She felt strange and scared. Surely, her brother loved her and would not let anything bad happen to her. Oh, how wrong she was! The little girl was raped by the whole gang. Most of the boys were in their teens, with her brother the youngest.

I was that little girl, scared and bewildered. I couldn't get away; there were too many of them. I couldn't outrun them; they were bigger than me. They didn't have any guns or knives but still, I knew I was their captive. After the attack, they warned me not to tell what had just taken place, saying "Something bad will happen to you." Their threats were enough to silence me for good, or so I thought.

But, to my surprise, the boys did talk! Several days later, at the same little country store, my older sister overheard some of the boys bragging about what they had done. She relayed what she had heard to our Mom, and I was called into the kitchen and told what the boys had said.

Forty-seven years after the fact, I can still see my mother as she reached into the wood box by the kitchen cook stove, took out a stick of firewood and beat me. Assuming I was guilty for letting it happen, she punished me. She didn't ask what had happened or why or how or when or who. I wasn't asked -- so I didn't tell.

I had heard all my young life that "Children are to be seen and not heard." So I never talked much, certainly not about anything so ugly. I suffered the pain in silence. No one ever mentioned the incident again in my presence.

I began to wet the bed. I was afraid of the dark. I had nightmares and was scared to death of snakes. It was not until many years later that I came to realize that all of these symptoms were normal responses to the kind of trauma I had suffered.

Some time later, I remember going to play with my best friend. After knocking, I was met at the door by her mother. I was told that I could not play with her ever again. I turned away without saying a word. I remember walking home sad. I never saw the girl again. I don't even remember her name. I guess her mother must have heard. Boys talk. Girls hurt. At least, I did.

We moved out of state shortly after the incident. I found a new girlfriend. We had fun playing together at school, but we lived too far apart to play after school.

Once, she invited me to spend the night at her house. I wanted to say "yes" but I was afraid that I would wet the bed and be embarrassed. I remember praying it would not happen if I spent the night. To my surprise, Mom allowed me to go for my first "sleep-over" with a friend.

We had such fun playing little girl games before and after dinner. She showed me her goldfish and we petted Sandy, her Cocker Spaniel puppy. Getting ready for bed was an apprehensive time for me because of my fears. After saying my prayers, I pled silently for additional help. No one else knew that the little girl was petitioning Jesus, "Help me not to wet the bed." When I awakened in the morning, I discovered that I was dry and so were the sheets on the little twin bed.

It was the first time I could remember sleeping between two crisp, white sheets. We had sheets made of feed bags at our house, and I didn't know there were any other kind until I spent the night with Cindy. I was so proud of myself! That was the beginning of the end of a struggle to gain back control over that embarrassing nightly occurrence.

Still, the guilt continued. There is a misplaced guilt for the victim. I was never "good enough," somehow dirty, unclean, unholy. "IT MUST HAVE BEEN MY FAULT." Yet, I didn't know how.

I bluffed my way through life. I did twice as much work to "pay" for what had happened to me. I volunteered for everything. I put on a mask and tried to please. I wanted to be liked. I felt I was always at the bottom, clawing my way to the top. I prayed that God would forgive me for what I thought was MY sin, but never felt He had. After talking to God about it, I would go around to the back door and say, "Give it back to me, Lord. Surely you can't forgive anything so ugly as that!" At least that is what I thought. I really was a "GOOD LITTLE GIRL," but I never felt like it.

I had assumed that when I was baptized at the age of 10, those awful feelings of self-hate and guilt would disappear magically. On that Tuesday evening, I recall being happy for the first time in more than two and a half years. But when I stepped out of the baptistery, though I loved Jesus, still I carried guilt that was not mine. I was hiding a secret that I believed He could not forgive.

When I was thirteen, my father also violated me. My baby sister and I had been left in his care while mother and our brother went to the Cherry Blossom Festival in Washington, D.C. On the pretense of kissing me good-night, I was maneuvered into an inappropriate situation. I felt his hands on my body and hard kisses with whiskers on my mouth. I found myself trapped again, for what seemed like an eternity. At last managing to make an excuse that I had something to do, I got away. But it was not without being scared for the rest of my life and losing trust in my father.

As a teenager, I made up my mind that I wanted to marry a minister. A minister was the closest to a heaven-bound person I could visualize. I never felt "good enough" to get to heaven and being married to a minister was the only way I could imagine seeing heaven.

My girlfriends thought I must be crazy. They surely would not dream of such a thing, and lost no time telling me that they would not be able "to keep all the rules." I guess they thought they had to be perfect, but what they didn't know was that I was going to rely on my husband to be perfect for me. My young mind had confused a lot of facts and this was another to add to the list. But I didn't know then that the only way to be saved is through the blood of Jesus. Through Him, I can be saved, I can be clean. Even a God-fearing husband cannot save me.

I came to the realization that I was not to blame. I was the victim. I was the one who was hurt, and hurt I did, for almost 41 years. It was not until the spring of 1989 that I told the most important person on earth: my best friend, my husband, that kind, loving, southern, gentle man that I had married 30 years before.

We had gone out of state for a chaplain's meeting. I thought this would be a good time to talk to him, while we were away from home. However, throughout the week there were meetings, lectures, and more meetings. Back in the hotel room, we had to change clothes for the next appointment and head out again. When at last the activities of the day were over, I was exhausted. Never once did I find an opportunity to tell John what I had hoped to get out. We came home without me making the disclosure I had planned.

After arriving home, I wanted to repack the suitcase and go to a motel. John couldn't understand. He thought it would be a foolish waste of money. My thought was to tell him this dreaded secret at a motel - anywhere, just so it was away from home - and leave it there.

❧ ❧ ❧

"Honey," I said, "I have something to tell you but I want your undivided attention." You see, John is a person who never wastes time and is always seen doing two things at once. Reading, sorting, filing or doing wood-working, while watching a TV show or waiting for an appointment. Every minute is accounted for. But I wanted him to concentrate only on what I had to say. Since he could not understand, I asked him not to have any book in his hand this time and just listen to me. He agreed.

I had never been able to share with him the pain and shame I felt. When I did, the healing began. Never before in my life had I verbalized the incidents. My ears had never heard my voice admit out loud what had happened to me. It took what seemed like hours to get the words out. There were long minutes of silence when the only sounds were those of sobs as I washed my soul with tears: tears stored up for many years. More tears than words came until I had emptied it all out. I told him not to ask questions, just let me tell him in my own time and my own way. He waited patiently with his arms around me as my body shook in uncontrollable weeping. Before the box of tissues was empty, I begged him not to hate me, and forgive me for not telling him before we married. I thought he wouldn't love me if he knew. And I desperately needed someone to love me.

He cradled me in his arms and said, "Honey, there is nothing to forgive. You were the one who was hurt. It was not your fault! I'm just sorry that you suffered so long and so needlessly."

Here I was a grown woman, forty-nine years old, and I had never heard anyone tell me "It was not your fault!" Hearing him say it made me realize for the first time that *it was not MY shame.* I had no part in it except in being so trusting and being in the wrong place at the wrong time.

John held me and prayed for me. That very hour, my healing began. I found cleansing for the first time. My world was different.

13

You know how it looks after a rain storm, when the rain has washed all of the pollutants from the sky. You can see for miles because the atmosphere is clear of all dust clouds. The tears had washed all the ugliness and guilt from my eyes and soul. Christ had lifted the darkness.

Some authorities say that sexual encounters between siblings should not be considered incest unless there are at least four years difference in age while others say two years. Regardless, I never felt the anger toward my brother that I did toward my father who was supposed to protect me. My father died thirty-five years after the incident, but still, I could not cry.

Because I had been beaten following the gang rape, I had stifled all of my emotions. When Dad violated me, my trust in him was suddenly shattered and when he died, I had no tears to shed. I was sad because the rest of the family was grieving for him, but I felt no grief. They did not know what I knew, and I thought I would never tell them.

My tears did not return until I began to deal with the abuse. Ambivalent feelings overtook me. The love/hate relationship left me numb. I loved my father, simply because he was my father and the only Dad I had. There were many things I admired about him and I knew he loved me too, in his own way. He never mentioned the incident that occurred when I was thirteen, and neither did I.

Once I began to deal with the abuse, I was asked, "Did your father ever apologize to you?" In his own way he did, but not directly. In his eyes, I was the best at anything I set my head and hands to do. He was constantly bragging on the jobs that I had done. He complimented my sewing, cooking, singing, and leadership. He bragged to anyone and everyone who would listen. I'm sure he was truly sorry, but he did not know how to express it.

The tears returned with my healing; tears for the little girl and tears for a broken relationship with my father who was, without doubt, also a victim of a hurting childhood; and tears for my own small son who never heard words of comfort following his abuse.

And after the tears, I knew that inside of me was a pearl waiting to be discovered.

2

Abuse And Oysters, Pearls And Healing

Several years ago, I became really involved in the study of sea shells. I was fascinated by the variety of colors, shapes and sizes, from the smallest to the large "giant clams." On family vacations, we picked up shells at the ocean, but they were usually inferior or all alike, depending on the time of day we happened to be out. Since we were never at the right place at the right time, we were not fortunate enough to land treasures like people who live nearby. Looking through shell books, I found that our collection was far short of the many varieties and certainly, less attractive. We had a lot of some and none of others.

During this time, I was teaching a class of teens at church. The theme for that quarter was "Lessons from the Sea." Each week, I would take along some shells so the youngsters could get a glimpse of the magical creatures from the deep.

Glancing ahead through the upcoming lessons, I realized that our collection was greatly lacking in some of the varieties that I needed. Since we lived in middle Tennessee, far from any ocean, I could have despaired except for one thing: Our youngest daughter lived in Florida, and since I was going through the empty nest syndrome, we visited her a lot. On the trips back from the sunny south, I would bring back shells. Some, we had picked up from the beach, but the collection was still not complete, so I did the next best thing. I would find myself wandering through shell stores. There were many really big and pretty shells to choose from. Shopping is an expected part of vacations. I didn't need dishes, clothes, shoes or trinkets from the tourist traps. Shells, however, I purchased with the great care I would use when picking out fine china. On those trips, I went into a lot of shell shops. It became quite a joke between my husband and daughter. "If Mom is missing, just look in the nearest shell shop!"

Once I found myself in a store called "The Pearl Factory." This shop sold really ugly but unique and special shells, and I just had to have one. Sealed in a plastic, see-through can, it was an ugly oyster! It was really nothing to brag about: just a dull, dark, grayish shell. Here was an opportunity for the teen class to experience the wonder of finding a pearl. Of course I bought it! After returning home, I could hardly wait for the week to talk about pearls!

At last, the day came. We talked about the many kinds of oysters, what they look like, how they eat and where they live. Some oysters are raised for food. They are not the same kind that produce pearls. Pearl oysters live in warm, tropical seas. Experienced divers can detect which oysters might contain pearls. Even then, many hours are spent diving and many oysters have to be opened to find an occasional perfect treasure.

Kokichi (coke-i-chi) Mikimoto was only a child when his father died. Eleven year old Mikimoto took over the family noodle business to support his mother and siblings. After working long and hard, he became successful and was looked up to by the business community. Because of his prestige in the business world, he was married to the daughter of a noble family.

As he became more prosperous, he traveled like a successful businessman. On one of his trips, he visited the Yokohama harbor. It was there that he saw pearls for the first time and fell in love with them. Besides the noodle business, he began to study oysters and pearls. He spent more time "playing with his oysters," and less in the factory. Soon, he put his wife in charge of noodles while he devoted his whole time to the study of pearl farming.

The business community, who had formerly praised Mikimoto for his success in industry, became disappointed. Their scolding, teasing and laughter could not persuade him to give up his love for pearls. He experimented for fifteen years before learning the secret to perfect pearls. He discovered that by placing a tiny piece of nacre (Mother-of pearl) from another oyster

16

and a small bead inside a host oyster, it would encourage the oyster to produce a perfect gem. The small bead was made by taking a large shell, like a conch, and grinding out small, round beads. This would insure perfectly formed pearls each time.

All pearls begin with a foreign object inside an oyster shell. In an effort to be able to tolerate the irritant, the oyster covers it over with layer after layer of shell-like material produced by its own body. In time, the foreign object becomes smoother and is no longer an irritant. Until Mikimoto's discovery, the irritant was usually a sharp and irregular grain of sand. Because so many oysters had to be harvested to find a usable one, the price was understandably high. Now, with Mikimoto's method, perfect pearls could be produced predictably. Mikimoto discovered he could make a very small bead from larger shells, especially conch shells. This bead was smooth and round and would guarantee a perfectly formed pearl. With this small bead and some tissue from another oyster placed into the oyster shells, success was likely within two and a half to four years.

It was with this guarantee that I had purchased the see-through can. After telling the young people the story about this interesting person, we went to the church kitchen and opened the can. With the class gathered around, we lifted out the oyster and proceeded to open the shell. Wide eyes peered in anticipation for the first glimpse. Oohs and Ayahs were the first responses as it was spotted. There, in that ugly shell, besides the dead animal, was our expected treasure. What we found was a most beautiful pearl, so creamy white, so round, so beautiful, and so perfect! The class followed the instructions of cleaning it first with salt and then with fresh water. They each took turns holding and admiring it. "Is it worth a lot of money?" they wanted to know. "Well," I said, " only about the ten dollars that I paid for it in the can."

We, as victims of sexual abuse are very much like that oyster. We often feel ugly and "clam up" to cover our pain. Year after year, we hide the pain and hurt in silence. But IF THERE IS HELP, someone to BELIEVE IN AND LISTEN TO US, we can come out of that ugly shell. Then you will see the beautiful pearl that has been born out of the ugly life we have been surrounded by. Are these pearls valuable? You bet they are! These pearls are bought with the sacrifice of the most valuable Child ever born on earth, the Pearl of Great Price. Jesus gave His life to redeem us from the clutches of Satan. While here on this earth, He too was bruised and abused. If we will only give Him a chance, He will put back the smiles that were stolen by our abusers.

Joel 2:25 reads, "I will repay you the years that the Locust have eaten." God can make BEAUTY out of ASHES, and PEARLS out of ugly OYSTERS.

There are hurting people all about us, in the church and in the community, men and women who have been abused. We must **heal the hurts** by speaking gently and with understanding.

Luke 12:48 says "Unto whoever much is given, much is required."

"Blessed be God, the Father of mercies and the God of all comfort; who comforteth us in all our tribulation, that we may be able to *comfort others who are in trouble,* by the comfort wherewith we are comforted by God," II Corinthians 1:3, 4.

After finding the healing for our souls, we can be a blessing to others who have experienced the same hurts. But some feel vulnerable because of shame. We have insisted on carrying the shame that does not belong to us. We must give it back to the abuser to whom it does belong and accept our freedom. Shame is no longer a weight to hold us down. Silence is what the abuser has counted on for so long. As long as the victim remains silent, the abuser is safe. Are we going to do them that favor for the rest of our lives? I think not! The abuse was not our fault and we should treat it just that way. Too many hide behind counselors' doors for confidentiality, all the while letting the abuser go free. Hundreds of thousands of dollars are spent on counseling. What for? To remain silent? Is it necessary that we live with the life sentence of shame from sexual abuse while the abuser goes free, with no responsibility for our therapy and pain? Confidentiality is nothing more than silence! Is this a gift that they deserve or one we can afford to give?

If a thief breaks into your house and destroys your furniture and personal things, your first wish is that he be caught. You call the police. They come and lift finger prints, gather clues, and file a report. The search is on. Before long, the thief is caught, charged and sent to jail.

What if you had not reported the crime? What if you had been quiet about it? What if you had insisted on confidentiality? The thief would not have to pay for his crime, and would remain free to break into your neighbor's home. Meanwhile, you live in fear that he may return. His crime belongs to him, not you!

When you have been sexually violated, it is the abuser's crime and not yours. Yet, it is the least reported crime. The more time goes by without reporting it, the less chance of having evidence to confront him. The "fingerprints" have been smudged, the clues become fuzzy and there are no records in the police reports that it happened, and you live in fear that he will strike again.

It is time we recognize sexual abuse for what it is: **CRIME.** It is a crime committed **against** you, not your crime or shame. We can no longer allow abusers to go free. We can no longer afford to protect them from facing their crimes and their shame. It does the abuser no good to allow him to remain free of guilt. His shame is safe while you keep his secret. Our secrecy only assures that he will continue his practices and not receive help for his sickness. It also delays our own healing process.

Repairing the damage done to the home that has been ransacked must take place before we can entertain guests again. Repairing of the destruction to the shattered life is necessary before we can trust again.

If the thief is not caught, he will strike again and again; in your neighborhood, your sisters' homes, your children's or grand-children's homes. If the abuser is not stopped, he too will strike again and again; in your neighborhood, in your sisters' homes, or in your children's or grandchildren's homes.

I found a bumper sticker that read, "It is never to late for a happy childhood." Unfortunately, it is not so. Someone has said, "A lost childhood is vanished forever!" How true that is! We can do some fun things in our adult lives to make new memories, but we can never regain those lost years.

Too many children are denied real love in the home. We have become a nation of unloved and unprotected children! These little ones are not taught physical or emotional boundaries for their own safety. They are being destroyed because we have not taught them how to protect themselves. We must be a safe person for our children to talk to. We must give them permission to talk about the "bad secrets."

It is no longer necessary to hurt in silence. Come out of that ugly oyster shell. We need to see the pearl. We need to hear the pearl. The silence is over!

I learned something else about the pearl. In order for it to retain its luster and life, the pearl has to be touched. The natural oils from the human hand and body are what give it life and beauty. Without these touches, the pearl will become dull and lifeless. After sitting on a shelf or in a drawer for a long time, the pearl will cease to reflect light and the colors of the rainbow.

We are all very much like the pearl. We need the touch, the hug and the smile from people who care about us. We need touches that convey "You are loved" and hugs that say "You are special." We need smiles that say "I really care."

In general, children receive only one positive touch to six negative touches in a 24 hour day. It is no wonder children feel unattractive and unloved! One psychologist said, "The number one problem in America is *unloved children*." How true! In 1991, there were two million reported cases of child abuse and neglected children. The numbers seem to grow each year. Where is the stopping place?

Unless we unite our efforts in education and prevention programs, children's lives will continue to be destroyed. Small pearls should not be lost in a sea of hopelessness.

3

Incest And Sexual Abuse In Biblical History

(Ancient Pearls)

Leviticus 18:6-23 *(Today's English Version)*: "The Lord gave the following regulations. Do not have sexual intercourse with any of your relatives. Do not disgrace your father by having intercourse with your mother. You must not disgrace your own mother. Do not disgrace your father by having intercourse with any of his other wives. Do not have intercourse with your sister or your stepsister, whether or not she was brought up in the same house with you. Do not have intercourse with your granddaughter; that would be a disgrace to you. Do not have intercourse with a half sister; she, too, is your sister. Do not have intercourse with an aunt, whether she is your father's sister or your mother's sister. Do not have intercourse with your uncle's wife; she, too, is your aunt. Do not have intercourse with your daughter-in-law or with your brother's wife. Do not have intercourse with the daughter or granddaughter of a woman with whom you have had intercourse; they may be related to you, and that would be incest. Do not take your wife's sister as one of your wives, as long as your wife is living. Do not have intercourse with a woman during her monthly period because she is ritually unclean. Do not have intercourse with another man's wife; that would make you ritually unclean. Do not hand over any of your children to be used in the worship of the god Milcom, because that would bring disgrace on the name of God, the Lord. No man is to have sexual relations with another man; God hates that. No man or woman is to have sexual relations with an animal; that perversion makes you ritually unclean."

Deuteronomy 27:20-23 *(Today's English Version)*: "God's curse on anyone who disgraces his father by having intercourse with any of his father's wives. And all the people will answer, 'Amen!'

God's curse on anyone who has sexual relations with an animal. And all the people will answer, 'Amen!'

God's curse on anyone who has intercourse with his sister or half sister. And all the people will answer, 'Amen!'

God's curse on anyone who has intercourse with his mother-in-law. And all the people will answer, 'Amen!'"

Incest is defined and strictly forbidden from ancient times. Apparently, mankind had a history of abusing its young, making necessary these regulations. Only now are we beginning to uncover the extent of sexual abuse to children and the damage it has done. All of the choices we make in adulthood result from a good or bad childhood. With sexual abuse so widespread, is it any wonder we see so many bad choices and messed up lives?

"Eighty-one percent of convicted child molesters were themselves molested as children. Seventy four percent of adult females studied who were molested as children report sexual dysfunction as adults."[1]

Are you now getting a glimpse of the long-term effects of this malady. Even during his lifetime, the "Father of Psychoanalysis," Sigmund Freud, did not realize the full import of what he was hearing from his clients. Incest and sexual abuse of children seemed so repulsive to his generation that he ignored the revelation rather than "expose the stink." He was given one of the first looks into our dysfunctional society, but covered it up. Men and women would have thanked him for exposing the secret over one hundred years ago. Instead, he is known for perpetuating the belief that victims somehow "asked for it."

Men and women are only now beginning to speak out on their own. Someone has suggested that the current campaign to expose incest, sexual abuse and harassment may be one of the positive ripples from the women's movement. Whether or not it came to light from women crying for equality, I am glad someone gave us permission to say, "We are not going to take it any longer!"

Because children are so trusting of their parents, guardians and caretakers, they are vulnerable to believe anything an older person tells them.

Colossians 3:20 *(King James Version)*: "Children obey your parents in the Lord." The key words are "in the Lord." The picture of marriage should be, if drawn geometrically, a perfect triangle with husband, wife and the Lord, each one with equal space, respect and voice. If parents are not behaving in a Christ-like way and are treating their children wrong, children will become confused. There is a spiritual warfare going on for control of the child. Satan sees no better way to destroy the family and increase his army of evildoers than to attack our young.

When respect for womanhood is uppermost in the home, incest is less likely to occur. If a man refers to his wife as "my old lady," or "the old woman," God is grieved. When we allow women or little girls to be only seen as bodies and sex objects, the creator is dishonored.

As young boys are molested, they are unconsciously being taught to be pedophile, rapists, homosexuals and wife beaters. These small male children are not given a chance at happy, carefree childhood--only a heart filled with shame and anger. The ones who hide their pain and shame are more apt to do these things as older children or adults. The Savior weeps when He sees His children treated this way.

Homosexuality and pedophilia were apparently two of the reasons that God chose to destroy the cities of Sodom and Gomorrah. Genesis 19:4-5 describes a sex-crazed mob of males, "both young and old." These young boys had already been perverted by homosexuals. Our word, sodomy, comes from the old testament city that practiced homosexuality. This gay mob surrounded Lot's house, demanding that his guests be brought "out to us so that we can have sex with them."

As we review the texts at the beginning of this chapter, we see that incest is not a new problem. God was displeased then! He is displeased now! Here we are, many thousands of years later, and either our forefathers didn't read the counsel or didn't heed the warnings.

Through the ages, if mankind had been caring for its children as originally planned, we would see only isolated cases of child abuse. Instead, we are suffering an epidemic! There has to be an all out war with sin and evil. The warriors are steadfast, the conquerors are many; the territory is great and time is running out. Only as we all join in the battle, will victory ever be in sight. In reality though, the battle will only be over as we are rescued from the planet. Every battle fought, every child saved, every adult restored, is a victory to be known only in the New Earth.

"Notwithstanding that the sins of a guilty world were laid upon Christ, notwithstanding the humiliation of taking upon Himself our fallen nature, the voice from heaven declared Him to be the Son of the Eternal. John had been deeply moved as he saw Jesus bowed as a suppliant, *pleading with tears* for the approval of the Father."[2]

The sin of child abuse is so repulsive, can you hear Christ *pleading with tears* to His father? He says, "This thing is so stinking, so vile, so repulsive, can you see through all this filth and accept my sacrifice for the sin? Can you really forgive them? Father, I know it is bad. It makes me so sad. Can you do anything about it? Will you accept my sacrifice?"

We know that God hates sin but loves the repentant sinner. Only in Christ is there hope for healing. And only in Christ can the evil be pardoned.

Endnotes

1. Daniel L. McIver, "Incest Treatment Strategies," in a paper presented to the Washington State Psychological Association, Seattle, Washington, 1984, page 15.

2. "Desire of Ages," by Ellen G. White, page 112.

4

Then Came VOHC

(Emerging Pearls)

Sunday morning, August 20, 1989, the Women's Ministries Executive committee met at the conference office. The major item on the agenda for the day was to plan for our first women's retreat in October. Kay Kuzma had agreed to be our speaker. Now we had to decide who would take care of other things that would make for a spiritually uplifting weekend. It was not long before we had a volunteer to arrange all of the music. Decorating would be fun and a committee was quickly formed to create an attractive setting. Registration, dining room hostesses, T-shirt and activities committees soon took shape too. Devotionals were assigned to various ladies, including myself.

It became my privilege to do the lay-out for the stationary and a logo for the posters and T-shirts. We wanted to make this first retreat an extra special weekend and having shirts alike would draw us closer.

Everyone had a job to do. With the air filled with the excitement about an outstanding retreat in October, we left for our homes.

As I headed my car toward Portland, I thought about the devotional I would give. We had an allotted time of eight minutes. Surely that could not be so hard. A topic was to be decided and assigned by the time the brochures were printed.

After I told John that whole ugly story of the sexual abuse, I remember he told me something that changed my life. The morning following the disclosure, he came to me and said "Honey, I'm glad you told me about the abuse. What you do with it now is up to you." That remark gave me freedom. I knew he loved me even though he had never really known me. Thirty years of living, eating and sleeping with me was not enough to actually know who I was. I had been afraid to share the pain and shame that had kept my mouth silent, my heart aching, and my body rebelling, because of the repressed guilt and shame.

From time to time in our ministry, parishioners had come to my husband for counseling about these same types of issues. He felt handicapped. Having been raised in a happy, not too dysfunctional home, he could not relate to what he was hearing. He gave the usual "Turn it over to God, stay out of reach, and forgive and forget," reply being taught in colleges and seminaries. No one was talking about sexual abuse much. It was considered a rare occurrence, and given very little attention. Women and men were still being silent about their abuse, yet exhibiting all of the symptoms of a childhood gone wrong. I took John's remark, "what you do with it now is up to you," as his call for help in this area which he knew little about.

The retreat devotional was on my mind. "What," I questioned, "would I talk about?" Remembering his remark gave me the courage I needed to go public. Within a few days, I was back at the conference office about another matter. Passing down the hall, I stuck my head into Mrs. Shankel's office. "Mabel," I said, "I think for my devotional at the retreat, I need to tell a story about my childhood abuse and the healing that has taken place just recently. I feel there are other women that may relate also. Eight minutes will not be enough time though."

She suggested "Let's talk to Sandy about it. Maybe we can squeeze a few more minutes in for you by cutting a minute here and there, but we do want to stay within our time schedule." Within a few days, I was on the phone to Kentucky, giving Sandy my request.

"Sharon," she replied, "that sounds like it would be a subject that would be helpful to many of the women in our church. In the news, so many people are talking about it these days. There are probably more women affected than we can imagine. We will arrange a few minutes more so you can do it. I've been

26

thinking more about the theme for the retreat and we have decided on `OUR GIFTS TO JESUS.' You know: our time, our talents, our praise, and our hurts. Your topic can be `Giving our hurts to Jesus.'"

If we are to believe what we read and hear in the media, sexual abuse is mostly a female issue. (Since that time, I have learned different, but that will be discussed in greater detail in the chapter titled "Yes, Big Boys **DO** Cry!") But for the time, speaking to a group of women seemed like a safe place for me to start.

The closer it got to October, the more I began to put my thoughts on paper. After working with it for a few hours, I sat down at the computer and typed four double spaced pages. I could read it in the twelve minutes that Sandy and I had finally agreed upon.

After doing the last minute editing, I laid a copy of it before John to read. "I'm going to talk about this at the retreat next month." Then I asked, "Will you be embarrassed with it?"

His reply gave me the assurance I needed: "Of course not! I believe you just may help some other ladies."

That was one hurdle down, two more to go. By then, our daughters were grown and living on their own. They didn't know! What would they think? Would they be disgusted with me? Would they hate their grandfather and uncle?

Knowing that Angela, our younger daughter, would soon be in Chattanooga for a wedding, I gave her a call. "While you are in, will you have some time for me? I want to bring Teresa down because I need to talk to both of you about something important." We agreed when and where to meet and that she would find a private place to talk.

Then it was time to approach our oldest daughter. Teresa was married and had a five year old girl of her own named Cassie. "Teri, can you go with me to Collegedale next Sunday? I need to talk to you and Angela about something."

David, our son-in-law, has a tendency to be suspicious. He wasn't too sure about the whole thing, and had conjured up his own reasons why he thought we wanted to be alone together, just us girls. I told him "David, please trust me on this." He tried, but it did not stop his active imagination: "What if I don't like the Christmas surprise you all are planning?"

Teresa and I left early Sunday morning, September 18th, for a one day trip. Along the way, we talked about Cassie, their house, my job, the new garage her dad had just built, and the horses along the highway. I guarded the true purpose of our trip as the miles sped away.

After greeting Angela, the three of us headed for a restaurant and had our fill of Mexican food, our favorite. I paid the check and we piled back into the car. "Let's go to the park near the college, Mom" Angela said when I looked to her with a question in my eyes. She told us all about the wedding, how pretty Kristy looked in her gown and how anxious her mother was.

Within a few minutes, we reached our meeting place. "Not too many here," I mused as I stopped the car and removed the key from the ignition. It was a little too cool for picnicking, so we had the park pretty much to ourselves. Spotting an isolated table, we headed that direction. The concrete bench was cool, which only added to my shaking as I contemplated how to reveal my secret.

I began the announcement by telling them I had something to tell them that I wanted them to hear from me rather than someone else. Tears interrupted the story almost as much as they did when I told it to their father.

By the time I finished, my daughters had their arms around me. This time, I was the child and they were the parents. "Mom, we are sorry you have hurt so long and never felt you could tell anyone. We love you." They had questions about how I could forgive and they felt anger toward their grandfather and uncle, as I had expected they would.

"I wanted you girls to know about this first. After the retreat, it will be public information that your mother is a victim of childhood rape, sexual abuse and incest." With the purpose of our rendezvous complete, we threw rocks into the creek like we had when they were little, then headed towards the home of friends. After visiting, laughing and exchanging craft ideas, Teresa and I decided it was time to start for home. Angela would be flying back to Orlando the next morning.

One month later, I shared the story at the retreat. "I'm telling you this because I suspect that there are a lot of you who have experienced the same kind of hurting childhood," I began.

Afterwards, a swarm of ladies came to me saying "Thank you for sharing. . . I, too, was a victim. . . Listen to me. . . Help me!"

When I got home, my phone started to ring, letters began to fill my mailbox, each with the same request. "When can you start a support group?" I gave all kinds of excuses. Actually, they were very good reasons. You know the ones! "I'm too busy, I've never done anything like that before," etc. After all, I was working full time. With my health waning and my physical resources limited, I surely did not need to take on another job. We all remember how it was with Jonah when God gave him a job to do. Jonah made excuses to keep from going to Ninevah and actually went the opposite direction. I did too.

One day, I heard a song on a Christian radio station that went something like this: "I'll do what you want me to do, God. I'll serve on all the committees. I'll even tithe 11% . . . But please don't send me to Africa." I thought getting involved in this kind of ministry was tantamount to being sent to Africa. Only a few were speaking out on the subject. No one knew the language. It would be embarrassing and no one wanted to listen. But God kept sending people who asked for help, so I finally set a date to start a support group.

I called the president of the nearby hospital and asked for a conference room. Sitting at my computer, I composed an announcement inviting all victims of physical, emotional and sexual abuse, rape and incest to meet on February 21 at 7:00 P.M. Sending it to eight pastors nearby, all of whom I knew, I asked that it be run in their church bulletins for three weeks. I sat back and waited. On the night of the first meeting, fourteen brave people showed up, and VICTIMS OF HURTING CHILD-HOOD (VOHC) was born.

Since that day, I have had phone calls and letters and visits from other victims, affirming me, coming in for counseling and pleading for help. A seed was planted for a regular support group meeting, but I gave it only half a thought and went on with my busy schedule. But the words would not go away, the words that no one talked about: sex . . . sexuality . . . sexual abuse. I told the group that night that if they had told me a year before that I would be there that night, I would not have believed them. People had said to me, "write a book, start a support group." Emphatically, I said "NO! It's too big a job. I have no time. I would be too vulnerable." But after that night, I felt that my life would never be the same.

VOHC adopted a goal of ending the cycle of rape, incest and physical and sexual abuse of children, through every means available.

I asked the group, "Why do I believe I have something to say? I don't claim to be an authority. However, forty-two years of pain, shame and guilt caused me to keep my eyes and ears open to the hurts of others, and I have read extensively. As I listened to talk shows, tapes, seminars, and documentaries on television, I soon realized that I was not alone. Because I had a Bachelor of Science degree in psychology and counseling, I have been called upon for counseling through the years. Doctors frequently referred hurting persons to me, and being the wife of a minister put me in many counseling situations as well. The purpose of this group is to find support for our aching hearts." This was the first such group in the area. We represented all levels of coping. We began to help each other face our pain and shame together.

Since beginning this book, I have completed a Master of Divinity Degree in Spiritual warfare. I am finishing a Doctorate in Counseling Psychology with the major portion already completed. What I have found in all my studies however, is that the more we learn, the more there is to learn, but THE SEARCH IS ON!

5

I Said "Yes"...Without Thinking

(Pearl Diver)

Scripture: "For which of you, intending to build, . . . does not sit down first and count the cost?" Luke 14:28

When our own desires are considered, it is necessary to count the cost of what is going to be required of our finances and time. That would be the only way to approach a project if we really expected it to succeed.

However, when God calls, He already knows the investments involved. Financially, He knows what to do. All things are His. As He sees our faith, unselfishness and trust in Him, He will open to us the necessary resources, whether financial, physical or human. This is just what God did for me.

Whenever I had doubts about what I was doing or the direction I was going with "Victims of Hurting Childhood," God gave me something to assure me I was on the right track. Sometimes, it was a song on the radio or in church, a phone call, an unexpected check in the mail, or a person who had the gifts or talent for a specific need in the ministry.

I had thought at times, whether because of my health or the rejection of requests for grant money or the slow pace of the lawyer's office in getting VOHC incorporated, that I should not have let myself get involved in the ministry. The voice of doubt was that of Satan himself, who knew that the mission of VOHC would slow down or thwart his purpose of deceiving souls. He put one stumbling block after another in the way and only as I remembered "with God, all things are possible," was his taunting voice drowned by an answer to prayer. In God's time and in God's own way, He desires to lead.

31

I recall one particular time when the work seemed overwhelming. My husband had just been assigned to a new district. Getting settled in our new home posed a problem that I had not been confronted with before. I had made friends and contacts all across the United States and the world. All of a sudden, I knew they would not know how to reach VOHC. I knew I had to get out a newsletter to let all these people know how to contact me. God sent someone who volunteered to put the addresses into the computer for the mailing list. The list seemed endless and the task would have flattened me, but God knew what I needed and sent the right person to meet that need at the right time.

When VOHC was first conceived, I had no idea of all I was getting myself into. Never did I dream that I would be doing so much writing. When God gave me the job to do, I just said "yes". . . without thinking about what I would be called upon to do:

. . . Without thinking of the times I would be awakened from a sound sleep when my body and mind were screaming for rest after a tough weekend seminar, to answer a jangling telephone to hear a cry for help on the line.

. . . Without thinking of the long trips back and forth to the airport that my husband would have to make. He did not like me to hassle with luggage, boxes of seminar materials, parking the car and shuttling back to the terminal, so he insisted on being my chauffeur.

. . . Without thinking of the time it would take from his ministry to do this for me.

. . . Without thinking of the lonely nights I would spend away from him. Even surrounded by people who wanted to see me, I still missed my best friend. I am like an anxious bride waiting her cue to go down the aisle every time the plane touches down at Nashville International. The stewardess gives her rehearsed warning instructions, "please remain in your seats with your seat belts fastened until the captain has brought the aircraft to the gate and turned off the seat belt sign." Oh, I stay in my seat all right, but poised and ready to sprint for the door as soon as I hear that "bing" of the seat belt sign. My seat belt is already unfastened quietly and laying across my lap as soon as I feel all the wheels make contact with the runway.

. . . Without thinking of the notorious "airplane food." The vegetarian "meal" once consisted of one-half of an unripened papaya that resisted being cut with only the plastic knife that I had been armed with. Another time, a salad was brought for breakfast. Someone should tell Sky Chef that vegetarians eat everything other people eat, except for the meat. I've learned to pack Little Debbies, peanut butter crackers and some raisins in my briefcase for such times as these, especially if I have a lay-over of several hours at a major airport, to be followed by an airline meal of a wilted lettuce leaf with neatly arranged orange and grapefruit sections. That's great if you are thirsty, but by that time, my stomach is rubbing my backbone!

. . . Without thinking that I would have to run between planes at the Atlanta, Chicago or Dallas airports. Anyone who has traveled on planes knows the miles of corridors that connect the spider-web of terminals! If I have an appointment at a small town like Fayettesville, Arkansas or Marshfield, Wisconsin, the only way to get there by air is on a small commuter plane. The gate to board that "little jobby" seems like it is in another county from where the 737 docked. At times, I have to run in order to make it there on time. Learning to pack lightly has not only been an art but a necessity.

. . . Without thinking of all the hours I would have to spend on the phone assuring callers that there really is a way out of the pain. After processing all the shame, guilt and anger, there is a tomorrow with sunshine and fragrance; that someday there will be times that the abuse is not remembered as often and it will not have the control that it does in the present.

. . . Without thinking that the need would be so great that I would cry to God, "I need Help." And He would answer back in some marvelous way, but not always the way I expected. One Friday evening, I got a call from a friend who volunteered to travel with me at her own expense. How often I had longed

33

for someone who knew when to hand out things at the seminars, someone who would remember to register people as they came in, someone who could greet people and make them feel welcome. God sent me such a person in Dean. She is good for a hug for those who need it, has enthusiasm and a smile that will not quit.

. . . Without thinking of the times I would be asked "where was God in all of this? Why can't I trust Him? How can I believe He really cares?" I will never presume to know the answers to the "God questions" but I do know He does not want His children to be hurt. Satan is the father of lies and causes them to question God's love.

. . . Without thinking that the stories I would hear every day would bring me to the realization that the world cannot last much longer, lest mankind destroy itself and its children. Generation after generation of abuse has led to degradation, shame, poverty and ruin.

. . . Without thinking of how many times God would use me to help pick up pieces of broken lives and point them to a book or person who, with God's help, can super-glue the parts back together again.

. . . Without thinking of the hours I would spend sending advertising ahead of me to promote an up-coming seminar. Without thinking of the letters to write, the phone calls to return, the information to mail out, the trips to the post office and the cost of so much mailing.

. . . Without thinking about a need for a manager to make the ministry run smoothly or even of the thought of having, out of necessity, to charge organizations a fee for my travel and seminar expenses. It was certainly without thinking of having my voice on audio and video cassette tapes!

. . . Without thinking that people I had never met would know my name and the work I was doing. The calls from far and near to speak to this group or that club still amaze me. How could one little ten minute talk at a women's retreat cause such an avalanche of requests?

. . . Without thinking that I would be asking people for money to fund the needs of VOHC. It was without thinking that by resigning from a job with a modest annual salary, it would leave me totally dependant upon God to meet the needs of the ministry. But when I stepped out, I did not look back.

. . . Without thinking that publishers would be asking me for a book manuscript. In school, I was only an average student. High School grades were usually B's and C's. The only exceptions were my home economics courses which netted me A's every year and led to my being named "girl homemaker of the year" by the Daughters of the American Revolution in 1958. Conjugating verbs, diagramming sentences, writing necessary term papers and doing research in high school and College never prepared me for the thought of putting my life in a book. Writing had never crossed my mind, though I have two sisters who are both published authors. God answered another cry for help when He sent Judy, an English major, to type the book.

. . . By all means, it was without thinking that there would be a need to have anyone else help me in this ministry, out of necessity, relying on volunteers because there was no money to pay anyone. It had not crossed my mind that my husband and I would have to rely on his salary alone after ten years of being a two salary family. During the first ten months of being on the front line full time, I had given forty-two seminars without salary and only one honorarium that was put back into the VOHC account.

. . . Without thinking that I would have to shop with a list again and eating out at restaurants would, of necessity, be only occasional, regardless of how tired my body was.

. . . Without thinking that I would need the Lord more than ever in my life. I would have to depend upon Him to put words in my mouth to answer questions I had never considered. God would have to be my physician when I was on the road, to strengthen and sustain me.

. . . Without thinking that I would have to speak for hours at a time, sitting or standing when my chest was screaming for my body to lie down. The Great Physician has never failed me. After being away for three days at a time, I have to rest as soon as I return. Because of "stuffing" the pain for nearly 42 years, my body has begun to tell on me. Lupus and arthritis always leaves me in pain and bone tired. It has taught me that I am nothing and I can do nothing without Him.

I didn't count the cost. God did. I said "yes" without thinking because He had seen the end from the beginning and knew He needed someone to "speak for the children." I knew it was not the only time He had used a weak and timid person to be His mouthpiece.

I've come too far to turn back. Doors for the ministry are opening continually. There is no stopping now. And thus, the search for pearls has a new diver!

6

What Is Sexual Abuse, Anyway?

(Seeds of Pearls)

Whenever the subject of sexual abuse and incest comes up, there are people who don't believe that this sort of thing could happen to young children. To them, it seems physically impossible, emotionally improbable and socially inaccurate.

A mother of three once said to me, "I don't remember being sexually abused as a child, myself, but I am so careful, almost paranoid with my children. I won't let them out of my sight at church or in the market. Is this normal?" After talking with her briefly about her childhood, it was evident that her mother had been a protected and pampered woman. The father had done all the buying, even the underwear, for the family. "Did your father ever touch you at anytime?" I asked. "No, he never touched me or my sister, that I remember" She added, "As we were growing into puberty, our father insisted on seeing our breasts so he could buy us bras." "Honey," I said, "that is sexual abuse! Anything that makes you feel uncomfortable or embarrassed, is sexual abuse."

Just because the father had not physically touched her or her sister, she never recognized the abuse. Any invasion of privacy, whether by exposure, gestures, or explicit suggestions such as viewing pornographic materials, fondling, oral, anal, or vaginal intercourse, all constitute sexual abuse. You were a victim if you were exposed to any of these. If what happened to you makes you feel ashamed, embarrassed, want to hang your head, not make eye contact, or want to never see the person again, you were sexually violated!

A broad definition of abuse is any act that violates another person. Specifically, sexual abuse includes incest, sexual assault, molestation, fondling and rape. Further, it is inappropriate sexual contact with a child by an adult or an older child. These persons can be relatives, close family friends, trusted adults or a stranger who uses power to obtain sexual stimulation or satisfaction. Sexual contact with children can be accompanied by physical, emotional or verbal abuse. Sexual abuse uses threats, coercion, mental manipulation, force, guilt, trickery, traps, violence or bribery. Secrecy is a key issue.

Any overt or covert sexual advance or contact that makes the child feel uncomfortable or uneasy, constitutes sexual abuse:

PHYSICAL
-- Contact or penetration of vagina, anus, or mouth with penis, fingers or objects.
-- Fondling of child's genitals, breasts or buttocks.
-- Child asked to touch or stimulate the offender's genitals or breasts.

VISUAL
-- Exposing genitals or masturbating in front of a child.
-- Bribing a child to undress.
-- Watching a child dressing, bathing, or toileting.
-- Posing a child for sexual pictures.
-- Gestures or suggestive indications.
-- Exposing a child to pornographic materials.
-- Forcing a child to witness other people engaged in sexual acts.

VERBAL
-- Sexual remarks, put-downs or come-ons directed toward a child.
-- Sexual threats: "If you don't, I'll. . . " and "if you tell, I'll. . ."
-- Constant sexualization of the environment, such as explicit sexual talk or slang used in conversation.

To grow up feeling good about themselves, children must have positive physical and verbal touches such as hugs, pats, smiles and affirmations. They will explore and learn sexual information at their own pace if not pushed by adults while they are too young to assimilate adult information. With age, they will develop a vocabulary in order to relate or relay sexual information. The very instant sexual abuse occurs, emotional growth is stunted. Children do not have the knowledge or language to express what has happened to them. There are no words in the vocabulary of a three year old to tell what has happened except "bad" and "hurt." The little ones know it is bad but are not sure why. They are too young to understand adult sexual information, but not too young to trust the adult. Because they have no vocabulary words to express the confusing feelings, the children are silent. Since it involves their private body, shame sets in, then guilt.

Children only know they "don't like it." Most parents fail to give their children permission to come to them and talk about anything that makes them feel uncomfortable. Children are given no boundaries for their physical and emotional safety.

It is important to tell your children what could happen. They may be approached by someone, but they have your permission to say "NO!" Our children are taught to honor and obey Mom and Dad and respect older people. Be sure, in your instruction, that these little ones know they have the right to protect their own "boundaries." Teach them to memorize "My body belongs to me and no one has a right to touch it on private places." Tell them they have the right to say "NO" and run away from anyone that makes them feel uncomfortable and to tell and tell again until someone listens to them and helps them.

It is very important that this instruction be given to your children as soon as possible. I've had some parents say "Sure, I'll tell them when they are ten years old." I'm sorry Mom and Dad, but that is not soon enough. One half of all sexual abuse cases seen in hospital emergency rooms are children five years old and younger. Do you understand? Under five years of age! I recommend that the little ones be told in a simple way at least by age three. Let's not deceive ourselves. We are living in a land filled with violence, sex and sin. You, and you alone, are responsible for how your children act and react until they begin their formal education at age six or seven. If you wait until the child is five, it is already too late in many cases. What a shame to interrupt innocence at such a young age, but we have no choice except isolation and that can bring on another set of problems and suspicions.

Discuss with them "good and bad touches." Good touches are hugs, pats on the head, smiles and handshakes. Bad touches that children suggest are hitting, fighting, kicking, throwing sand and dirt. Tell them "Yes, those are all bad touches but another bad touch that makes you feel uncomfortable, unhappy or sad is a touch on your body where you wear your swimsuit or underwear. Any time someone tries to touch you on private places on your body, it is a bad touch. You don't have to let anyone touch you if it makes you feel funny or you don't like it."

Tell your child not to listen to anyone who claims the sexual thing they want to do is O.K. or normal. It is also important to explain that even adults or older children whom they know or even love, or those in authority such as baby-sitters, uncles, coaches, scout leaders, or relatives might try to approach them sexually. Children should be told that sexual abuse is *always* the offender's fault.

Teach your child not to keep "bad secrets." A good secret usually involves surprising and making someone happy but a bad secret is one that makes you feel sad. If anyone says "this is our secret," that is one they should come and tell you.

Warn your children not to accept gifts or bribes. Child molesters offer gifts or may try to trick them by offering money and presents for sexual favors. Tell them to always say "I have to ask my Mom or teacher first." This may deter a potentially dangerous encounter.

If the worst happens and your child is sexually abused, keep several things in mind:

40

1. *Be calm. Do not over-react or get angry.* I realize this is hard to do but your child has already been hurt. Do not hurt them further by your reaction. They will take the blame, thinking "It is my fault and now I hurt Mommy too!"

2. *Tell your child "What happened **was not your fault!*** You did nothing to cause yourself to be treated like that." Make sure they can say out loud to you, "It was not my fault." Their ears must hear their own lips say the words so they can believe it!

> "It was NOT MY FAULT!"
> "It was NOT MY FAULT!"
> "It was NOT MY FAULT!"

If we say it three times, it becomes a part of us. We own it. We can believe it. It is true!

It is the responsibility of the parents, teachers, and clergy to educate and protect children against child abuse, and to recognize behaviors and symptoms.

Physical and overt (open) sexual abuse are easy to spot. Physical symptoms, such as black eyes, bruises, cut lips, dental "accidents," broken arms and shoulders, etc. are possible indications of physical abuse. Overt sexual abuse may be kissing of a child on the mouth, fondling, and suggestive talk in public.

Covert abuse is "covered up," hidden, or subtle. "Subtle assassination" can include parental flirting, vulgar gesturing, telling dirty jokes or stories, relating sexual experiences in the presence of children, sexually stimulating behavior or environment, and put-downs. "Soul murder" is usually done by this type of abuse. Very often, this is when children are threatened with harm if they tell the offender's secret.

Other forms of abuse are more difficult to recognize. Mental and emotional abuse are more difficult for an outsider to spot. Unless time is spent with the victim, this abuse could go undetected. But comments like "Get lost," "I wish you had never been born," or "You can't do anything right!" cause permanent mental and emotional scars.

41

I grew up hearing the old saying, "sticks and stones may break my bones, but words will never hurt me," but emotional scars run deeper than physical injuries. Just ask a victim of emotional or mental abuse about the effects of carelessly expressed words. Even when abuse occurs, life is not over. Life can be full again!

Although my physical body had been raped as a child, I entered marriage as a virgin. What was done TO ME "was not my fault." There was no reason to feel like "damaged goods." The shoppers had handled me roughly and soiled the fabric of my outer self, but inside, I had reserved myself for a life-long companion. Thirty years into my marriage, I rejoiced over that realization. I had been a virgin bride!

7

Prevention

(Protecting the Pearls)

The first step to prevention is believing that it can and does happen. Admit that it is a real problem! Can you watch the six o'clock news and doubt that there is an epidemic in the land?

Learn to recognize symptoms and behaviors:

1. Does the child appear to be angry? Has he become a behavior problem at school, playground or church?

2. Is the child fearful of certain persons, situations or strangers? Does the child verbally declare he does not want to go to "his house" and shy away when around certain people?

3. Is the child's sleep disturbed by nightmares? Does he have dreams of being chased or caught? Does he feel trapped and helpless in his dreams?

4. Has the child become withdrawn socially or emotionally from family and friends? Is he isolated, saying "leave me alone?"

5. Has bed-wetting recurred in the child? Does he say "I had an accident" or "I can't sleep?"

6. Have there been personality changes in a formerly out-going child? Has the former leader become withdrawn?

7. Has the child become fearful of the unknown? Does he ask "what if the house catches on fire? What if Mommy has a car accident?"

8. Has the child suffered loss of appetite? Does he often say "I'm not hungry" or "I'm sick?"

9. Are there unprovoked crying spells? Does the child burst into tears when a significant parent leaves?

10. Is the child clinging? Does he say "please don't leave me?"

11. Does the child wash or bathe excessively or talk of feeling dirty?

12. Does the child say "I am no good" or "I can't do anything right?"

13. Are there changes in play? Is victimization and violence expressed in play?

14. Is the child fearful of the dark or being alone? "Don't turn out the light" and "don't leave me."

15. Does the child run away? Does he say "I don't like it here or does he look for safety?

16. Does the child display early sexual precociousness such as excessive masturbation? Does he use sexually explicit words or actions inappropriate for his age?

Be a safe person for your children to talk to. Always believe what the children say, regardless of how well you think you know the offender. Your children should feel free to talk to you about anything. If you do not know your children, you will not know when something is wrong.

Commit your children to God daily. Ask Him every day to place a protecting hedge of angels around your children. Even our God who loves us will not interfere where He is not asked. Many parents question "Where was God when this was happening?" "How can a God of love let a thing like this happen?" As an earthly parent, you hurt when your child hurts. The Heavenly Father sheds tears too. If something as bad as sexual abuse happens to your child, DO NOT BLAME YOURSELF OR GOD. Remember, we live in a world of sin and evil. God will help with recovery.

It is essential to provide proper sleeping arrangements for all family members. Be sure that the boys and girls in the household have separate beds and rooms. Doors should have working latches on the inside especially if a child is afraid.

When making decisions about day care for your children, understand the sexual response of some adults to children. A child may be in jeopardy even when left alone with an adult you believe to be safe. Look for the presence of an adult's previous problems and background. Consult with other parents and, by all means, get references and check them out. Ask about visitation policy and a schedule of activities.

Be careful about leaving your children alone with an adult or an older child in a private place, even if you think you know the person. Encourage the children to talk to you about what happens when they are with that person. If the child is uncomfortable with someone, listen carefully. They may be trying to tell you something, but do not know the right words to use.

Be suspicious of any adult or older child who pays unusual attention or spends too much time around children without good reason or accountability. Assure your children that they will be protected from anyone who makes any sexual advances toward them, but they must tell you what is going on. It is important that there be open communication between you and your children. Be sure they know they can trust at least one parent.

Visit the neighborhood library or bookstore for some books you can read and discuss with your children or let them read for themselves. Here are just a few books to look for:

---"Good Hugs and Bad Hugs" by Angela R. Carl
---"I Can't Talk About It" by Doris Sanford
---"Never Say Yes to a Stranger" by Susan Newman
---"No More Secrets for Me" by Oralee Wachter

There are many good books written especially for children. Find some and be armed with valuable information for your child's safety. Protecting these pearls is the sacred trust of all adults.

8

A Child Is Not For Hurting

(Rescue the Pearls)

Sexually abused children go through life accepting responsibility for happenings over which they had no control. They learn to cope in a number of different ways.

The first noticeable coping mechanism may be *withdrawal and silence*. If children who are normally outgoing become sullen and lonely, there is good reason to believe the children have experienced some emotional trauma.

Children may become *very active* in an effort to feel safe, constantly busy or running as if to say "they can't hurt me again if they can't catch me." Very active children will go from game to game, activity to activity, never stopping until becoming exhausted. These same children become adults who go from job to job, relationship to relationship, moving from place to place in an effort to find safety.

Another way to cope is to become *pleasers*. These victims attempt to do everything right so they won't be hurt again. They feel that something they did caused them to be hurt. These children never learned to say "no," and even as adults, continue the same pattern of coping. Problems of low self-esteem and never taking care of one's self are often evident in adulthood.

You may see very *angry* children trying to cope with the pain in the only way they know. They have been hurt and are very angry about it. These children may become controlling, aggressive, or even revengeful. You can see these children pulling the dog's tail or throwing the cat onto the house roof. They will get into fights on the playground, maybe even become the bully at school. "You give me your lunch money or I will beat you up after school." Their way of controlling other kids is to threaten and fight. These little ones are using the only skills they know to control the environment, and make things happen their way. Someone said it well: "A misbehaving child is a hurting child!" We, however, have looked at these children as discipline problems, delinquents or brats.

I saw something recently that pointed this out and made me cringe for the hurting child. Reading over some material that someone had given me for a girl's home, I stopped in my tracks. It referred to the applicant as a girl "with problems . . . she has become unmanageable, rebellious and failing in school." Doesn't the parent of this child know that the unmanageable and rebellious daughter is crying out for help and love? Instead, they were sending her away so someone else could "fix the problem."

Rejecting love in all forms is another coping mechanism for hurting children. These children may say "don't touch me," and shy away from any kind of hugs. They guard their personal property from intruders and invaders of their space. This is the only protection the children feel they have and it should be respected. These children grow into teens and adults who are unable to believe they are lovable. Often, they are told by their abusers, "No one loves you but me."

Abused children may cope by *shutting down emotions*. They may be unable to express emotions or feelings at the death of a close family member or pet. Often, children are told "do not cry" or "don't tell anyone." The threats that accompany these messages let the children know that it is unsafe. If someone sees them cry in their pain, an explanation would be needed. If the truth were told, the abuser would hurt them again, so they choose rather to be silent and shut out all feelings including pain, sadness, happiness, love and compassion. The expression of emotions was not permitted and through the conditioning of time, they soon forget how to feel.

Abuse may cause victims to *feel unworthy* of anything good, whether things or relationships. The victims do not feel "good enough" to have a happy relationship, pretty clothes or a nice home. These children become young adults who make bad choices in a marriage partner. They choose a mate who shows some of the qualities of their abuser. If a girl's father was an alcoholic, she probably chooses a drunk to marry. This girl does not know how to make good choices and does not feel she deserves anyone better. She may marry more than once, but always the same type of personality. She and her children are often the recipients of the rage following a drinking spree. This will cause her to leave and return again. If she does divorce the abuser to protect herself and her children, she falls back into the same trap in subsequent marriages, unless she can regain her self-esteem and realize she deserves better.

Children will deny the abuse to protect the offender and family members. SILENCE! "If you tell, something bad will happen to you." As young children, they believe it. "Mommy and Daddy will get a divorce and it will be *your* fault." They are just too little to accept that kind of guilt. "You will be taken away and put in a foster home." Years ago, children were put in an orphanage if they could no longer live with their parents for any reason. Or the children might be told "Daddy will be put in jail. You won't have a home if that happens." Their security is in jeopardy. Threats and guilt spell silence, thus protecting the abuser. The children are hurt over and over again because they are trapped by circumstances. Victims may become adults and still be protecting their abusers through their silence.

Suicide is not an uncommon method of coping. The victims feel the abuse has gone on forever and there is no way out. If they left, where could they go? If they told, no one would listen. A young girl may be pregnant with her father's child. She may take her life rather than face any more shame. Young girls and boys as young as seven have been known to commit suicide in order to escape the anguish of more abuse.

If children constantly *put themselves down*, we should hear another alarm of hurting children. They will say, "I'm no good" or "I can't do anything right. Nobody could love me. I don't deserve . . . " Because of the shame, these children cannot forgive themselves

48

and cannot see how God could love them. They stay at a distance from God, all the while wishing for a closer relationship. This attitude comes from low self-esteem and repeating the negative messages heard, "You are no good. . . a slut . . . ugly . . . evil, etc." Pay attention to this genuine cry for help.

Abused children will protect themselves by distance. They have become *unable to trust*. An adult or an older person whom they trusted has betrayed them, thus destroying the ability to trust again.

The same lack of trust is transferred to other individuals with whom the victims associate power or position, or who are of the same sex, age or occupation or have some other character-istic of the abuser. For example, if a girl was abused by a minister, all ministers are gùilty in her eyes. Because the minis-ter represents God, God is at fault. Church attendance is painful or out of the question altogether.

If the child was abused by a religious father or step-father, the anger is again transferred to God. "Heavenly Father" is not a pleasant or comforting thought to an abused person who had no positive role model for what a father should be.

Father's Day is not a happy or joyous holiday for victims of child abuse. Trust was betrayed and father should not be hon-ored, and rightly so.

Children are taught to honor their father and mother. Blindly, many children are led as lambs to the slaughter by that commandment. As we look at the New Testament, Paul explains it further in Ephesians 6:1: "Children, obey your parents *in the Lord.*" In other words, Children should obey their Christian, God-fearing, God-loving, God-obeying parents. If a parent asks a child to jump off a bridge, we know the parent does not have the child's best interest or safety at heart and neither is he a God-fearing parent. The trust is broken. Loyalty or obedience to a destructive parent is not in the best interest of the child.

In the winter of 1992, a young boy divorced his parents in a landmark legal case. His best interests had not been considered. His care and safety were not given proper consideration when he was placed in numerous foster homes and finally, a boy's home. His parents never visited. He had no family. He took his future into his own hands by divorcing his birth parents and choosing a family to be adopted into. He would no longer be bound to a family who did not love him. He learned to trust again.

Victims will learn to live with guilt and shame as another means of coping. While children are not for hurting, many a little heart is burdened with guilt. Always believing "It must have been my fault," they carry the guilt, believing they have caused their own pain and their dysfunctional family's pain. The "if only" mentality causes them to believe that circumstances could have been different: "if only I had done something" or "if only I had not been there or worn that. . . "

Besides children's own misplaced guilt, they are often told outright that it was their fault. Children believe older people and can not rationalize: "When is it ever *my* fault for *you* to hurt *me*?" They do not have the benefit of mature thinking at a young age and cannot sort fact from fiction.

There is another reason that some may carry guilt and shame. If, during any of the abuse, the children received even the smallest amount of pleasure or comfort, they will blame themselves, and feel shame. The normal reaction to stimulation of sexual organs is arousal. Voluntary or involuntary arousal will occur if stimulation is applied in vital places. Children may experience pleasure, even slightly, and then condemn themselves for taking part in the abuse. Following the rape, they may feel shame because of the pleasure associated with the stimulation. There may also be guilt because their body betrayed them if they were aroused.

Children may feel that this is the only time they are loved and accepted by this adult. Guilt swallows them because they endure abuse in order to feel loved.

Still another reason to carry the shame is caused by guilt over self-sex or masturbation. It is not uncommon for abused children to seek the same "good feeling" by themselves, but then guilt beats them down. As stated earlier, sexually abused children are "brainwashed" with adult information and later, the "bad" feelings of guilt cause them confusion.

Shame associated with self-sex destroys the mental health of a large number of children and adults and is at the root of sexual addiction. Guilt refuses to allow them to forgive themselves. Self-sex, shame and then guilt chase them around in circles because there seems to be no stopping place. Back-lash in this one area of guilt can lead to homosexual practices.

An attempt to *become invisible* is another trait that victims might exhibit. They may feel that others can see right through them, as if they were not even there. Children who have been victimized previously will tend to be shy, hang their heads, not look anyone in the eye, or become a pleaser. A pedophile knows what to look for and uses that knowledge to choose victims for exploitation. Unless trained in what to look for, most people are unsuspecting of signs and behaviors that victims are sure will make themselves invisible. Their constant putting down of self is the basis of low self-esteem. They feel, "If you really knew me, you would not like me," and "If I don't take off my mask, you can't get to know me and see that I am a bad person." The mask stays on, the games are played and the helper or pleaser personalities hide from others who they really are.

These children feel ashamed and will not look into the eyes when spoken to, for fear that you will be able to "see" guilt in their eyes. This is their way of hiding the truth from you or dealing with their own pain.

As mentioned, victims of sexual abuse have very low self-worth. Constantly putting themselves down and carrying misplaced guilt reinforces in their own minds, "I am no good, I can't do anything right and it is all my fault." This attitude refuses them the right to forgive themselves for being victimized. Feelings of low self-worth have blocked knowledge of innocence and not allowed recovery.

Another form of coping is creating a *pretend world*. Akin to wearing a mask, pretending helps children to cope. Play may be passive, showing happy, fun things and feelings, or it may be aggressive activity displaying anger. Always playing the clown is common among victims of abuse. Pretending is another way of forgetting, even to the point of blocking the memory of the abusive incidents.

In order to cope, children may *become perfectionists*. This is related to an earlier section on being a pleaser. The goal is not to make any more mistakes, to do everything "just right." These children may strive to make all A's in school, thinking it will spare them from "punishment." Keeping their room and belongings in order is a compulsion. Protecting their space is important. Locks and privacy are a very real necessity. Cleanliness can become a compulsion. Anorexic or bulemic tendencies may stem from a need to create and maintain a perfect body.

The results of this behavior however, tend to create a controlling person. The urgency of doing things "right" usually means doing them "my way." This trait in adulthood is likely to produce controlling, hard to get along with managers, whether in business, education or other professions.

The last means of coping that we will discuss is *hiding behind layers of clothing or wearing hair over the face*. This tendency stems from having no place to run and being trapped with no way of escape. Abused children may put on several layers of clothing, often inappropriate to the season, as a means of making themselves less accessible. They hope that so much clothing will discourage the abuser and cause him to leave them alone. If physical abuse has occurred too, long sleeved shirts and long pants can hide bruises until they heal. Wearing baggy clothing as a figure disguise is sometimes employed. Girls will often wear boy's apparel to discourage attacks.

One of the most unhealthy ways used to make themselves unattractive is to gain weight. A compulsion to eat and make themselves less attractive also lowers self-esteem or self-worth. The need is to be invisible or not seen or found attractive. Hiding in an unattractive body seems like a safe thing to do until they look in the mirror. Because of what they see, they avoid mirrors and self-esteem becomes non-existent.

I'm sure there are other ways of coping with abuse or variations of the ones we have discussed here. Each victim will employ several strategies in dealing with their hurt. A lifetime of coping ingrains patterns of behavior that will be hard to overcome during the recovery process. New thinking is necessary to break old ideas of what is safe.

Forgiving ourselves for carrying another's blame is the greatest gift we can give ourselves. Despite thinking the abuse was our fault and not being given permission to talk about it, many of us are only now giving ourselves the gift of forgiveness and total release from guilt. The coping mechanisms employed are no longer necessary. Though we see the reasons, we can look and even laugh at how our young minds chose to cope with adult shame in our child-sized heart. Pearls are rescued by the process of believing, understanding, helping, forgiving, and then rebuilding the broken pieces.

9

Yes, Big Boys Do Cry

(And Little Pearls Too)

When it was time for our youngest child to be born, Dorcas, our niece came to stay with our two little ones. Matt had just turned five on the 10th of April, 1965, and Teresa was fourteen months old. At age nineteen, Dorcas took to caring for our home and two pre-schoolers like a seasoned pro. Cooking, feeding and bathing the baby girl, making beds and washing diapers and bottles was soon a regular routine.

One day, as Dorcas busied herself in the mobile home, Matt ran into the yard to play and drive his blue pedal car. Morning passed quickly as she tended to the needs of the toddler and put her down for a nap.

Lunch was started but soon she realized there were no sounds of the little boy's "udden-udden" as he pedaled his blue car up and down the walkway. A sudden rush of panic overtook her as she realized there was no little boy in sight. She called to him -- no answer. Quickly running into the yard, she called his name over and over. She circled the residence. No answer came. No little boy appeared. Within moments, John arrived home from classes at the university. Noting the look of terror on her face, he joined her search. With a feeling of panic, he rushed to the busy highway, all the while praying for the safety of his child. At the edge of the highway, he stopped. There was no sign of the small, towheaded boy. Retracing his steps, John continued to call Matt's name. Still, there was no answer.

Beyond the last street of the mobile home park lay an open field with tall, dead grass from the previous fall and new spring weeds, as well. The grass was high, but not high enough to hide a very active and curious little boy. However, in the middle of the field was an old, dilapidated tool shed. The landowners had told us we could store things there that did not have to be out of the weather, since the windows were broken and the door was missing a hinge. The wind blew rain and snow through the openings. During the months we lived at the trailer park, we stored empty canning jars in the building. Matt had often gone with me to retrieve them, to use in canning the plentiful tomatoes and peaches.

As John made the turn and headed toward the shed, he heard the cries of a small voice. When he opened the door, he found Helen, the property owner's thirteen year old daughter, and our small son with his pants down. Matt was gathered up and brought back to the safety of his home, but nothing was ever done to the teenager. I was still in the hospital when John told me what had happened. It was not mentioned again.

It was not until twenty-seven years later that I realized what had happened to our son. The small boy had been sexually abused, and there was no one to speak up for him. I had not taken care of the seven year old girl who had been gang raped and later, molested by her father, and I could not take care of my only son. He was never told, "IT WAS NOT YOUR FAULT." As his mother, I did not yet recognize the need to deal with what had just happened to my own precious five year old boy. I could not give what I did not have.

In those days, silence was considered reasonable and accept-able, but not talking about it does not make it go away. I never related my son's behavior that I began to witness shortly after-wards, to what had happened to him on that fateful day. Matt became aggressive and controlling in some ways. That caused the rest of the family to assume he had inherited his mother's disposi-tion. In his youth, he displayed a certain distrust and aggression toward teen girls, although he was always compassionate and loving to small children and older persons. He was stronger than he realized and would get carried away in his rough-housing, often causing bruises. Once during play, he broke five of his father's ribs in a scissor hold, and felt badly afterwards.

55

He was a very compassionate child, and a friend to all he met. Yet, his heart carried a pain that I did not recognize until I looked back at his pictures and saw a pasted-on smile and hurting eyes that screamed "pain."

Four year old Donny scrapes his knee and elbow when he falls from his tricycle. Screaming, he limps to the door. He is met by his mom who, only minutes before, had hugged, soothed, kissed and bandaged seven year old Amanda's hurts. To him, she only says "Big boys don't cry. Don't be a sissy!" He can't understand why Amanda, his big sister, is shown compassion and he is met with disdain.

"Why doesn't Mommy like me today? Is it because I am so small and should not be so loud compared to my size? Maybe now that I am four, I'm big after all. Mommy said `big boy.' Does that mean I am a big boy? But my knee hurts. Can't Mommy see that? Does all this mean my sister is smaller than me? When did I grow up? Was it all at once? I'm still too little to reach a glass in the cupboard without climbing up on the counter, but too big to cry when I fall off."

No, Donny doesn't understand and neither do I. He is told he is too big to cry, but he's not too big to hurt!

Ever since I was a child myself, it always puzzled me when I was told I was not supposed to cry when something hurt. Even if I got spanked for being naughty, I was not supposed to cry about it. I wondered, "Don't grownups know it hurts when they spank me?" I thought that was the whole purpose of the punishment. All the time I was being whipped with a switch or a belt, I was told "shut up, don't cry." Having never been allowed to express my emotions at such an early age, I stifled the expression of physical and emotional pain. When I was sexually violated, I knew it was not safe to tell anyone for fear of being rejected again.

Some research figures tell us that one in every three adult females and one in every five adult males were sexually abused by their eighteenth year. Because men have been reluctant to admit to abuse and little boys have not had permission to talk about it, I have a feeling that those figures do not reveal the true picture. It is more conceivable that the statistics should reveal equal numbers of male and female victims.

At my seminars, I ask the gentlemen in the audience to finish a sentence for me. I say, "As a little boy, maybe three or four, when you fell down and skinned your knee, you were told . . . . " A chorus of male voices come back to me, "Big boys don't cry."

I have had only three men tell me they had not heard this while growing up. The first one was my husband. The second was a gentleman who contracted polio at age three. The third was a man who was not born in the United States.

As a victim of a hurting childhood myself, I had not dealt with my own pain. Therefore, I did not relate to Matt's behavior, and was not the support I could and should have been to a sexually abused boy. I too am guilty of telling my son what I had heard other mothers saying to their sons: "Big boys don't cry." After all, he was our oldest child.

There are several reasons that the "big boy" adult male does not cry for the little boy:

1. They have blocked out or suppressed their abuse. Males block out bad experiences just as often, if not more often than females. (Twenty percent of females have blocked memories.)

2. Thirty percent of the male population doesn't want to admit that sexual abuse happened because it would make them look weak or sissy.

3. They don't recognize all the faces of sexual abuse. (See the chapter entitled "What is Sexual Abuse, Anyway?")

4. Because their body responded to the stimulation, they felt they were at fault for the abuse and betrayed by their bodies. Child abuse is NEVER the fault of the child!

5. Because of the good feelings they had experienced, they may have begun to stimulate themselves, to re-experience the same feelings. Self-sex causes guilt and shame.

57

Therefore, this makes them deny abuse because of those feelings of guilt and shame. Self-sex or masturbation is not uncommon with children, both boys and girls, who have been sexually abused. Excessive or compulsive masturbation can lead to sexual addiction or homosexuality.

Little boys should be encouraged to talk about anything that makes them feel sad or uncomfortable. They should be informed by those they trust that there are some secrets that should not be kept.

If there were no sexually abused little boys, we would not have sexually abused little girls! This in no way excuses or lessens the impact of sexual abuse. I have learned a great deal from my clients. During recent years, as I have counseled with victims and abusers alike, one common fact has surfaced from these sessions. The abusers have been a victim of some kind of childhood abuse themselves.

Parents, our responsibility is to fulfill the child's request to "keep me safe." It should be understood that this is what parents should do, but we have failed miserably.

Yes, Big boys do cry . . . and little pearls should!

10

The Angel And The Accident

(Unrevealed Pearl)

My son's need for control and power was evident, even in his late teens. Fast, powerful automobiles became his passion. His cars were not only for transportation but prized possessions, something he could be proud of. The car would be washed, polished, cleaned, vacuumed and pampered. No empty soda cans or gum wrappers cluttered the floor. Once the car was in the driveway, it was ritually emptied of litter, dusted and polished almost daily.

Matt had just purchased a red Pontiac TransAm on the 13th of February, 1979. The following weekend, he planned a short trip to nearby Columbia, Tennessee with two of his friends. It had started raining early in the afternoon. The temperature dropped more suddenly than expected and the roads began to freeze, becoming slick in spots and making driving hazardous.

About 11:00 P. M., the phone rang. It was Matt. He and his friends were at the hospital. They had come upon one of those slick spots on a straight stretch of road. Unexpectedly, the car began to spin off the pavement onto the gravel shoulder of the road. The car flipped as it slid over a small slope, three to four feet high. The Red TransAm landed gently but suddenly on its top with the three young people inside, unhurt except for bad cases of fright and some minor scratches and bruises. The car was not so fortunate. Matt's pride and joy, broken, muddy and crumpled, had to be towed to a garage. There was broken windshield glass and car parts scattered along the edge of the road. The side windows did not break, keeping the car from crushing the young occupants. The three crawled out to freedom, basically unhurt, but the state trooper thought it wise for them to be checked out at the emergency room.

"Mom, Bud's dad is coming to get us in his truck. I'll be home in about forty-five minutes," Matt stated on the phone. Shortly after midnight, he walked through the door, a little downcast but no broken bones, casts or crutches. John and I told him how lucky he was to be alive. We felt grateful. The unexpected ice storm had caught us out earlier and we had seen others who would never return again to their home. We remembered praying for his safety when we saw he was not home when we arrived.

Monday morning, Matt called the insurance company and the garage. The insurance adjuster appraised the crumpled mass of metal and fiberglass. The verdict: total loss. After assessing the situation and contemplating the cost, Matt approached the insurance company. He bought back the wreck and had it towed to a body shop. Three months later, he drove it home, looking like a new car, minus the "fire bird" on the hood. His "baby" was back and given the same tender loving care as before. It took him to work in Lawrenceburg, Tennessee and Florence, Alabama, on dates, to visit his buddies and once to Memphis to see old friends he had left behind one year earlier.

One day in July, Teresa and I chatted as she sketched a horse from a photograph. She asked me when Matt was coming home from Alabama. He had left on Sunday afternoon to work in Florence for a few days. I glanced out the living room window toward the road at about 3:15 and saw Matt's car. As I watched, he passed the house and pulled into the lower driveway. I noticed he had someone with him. Turning to Teresa, I remarked "There's your big brother now and he has someone with him." With that, Teresa was up from the table, down the hall and down the stairs to greet them.

A few minutes later, Matt and Teresa ascended the basement steps. Matt went into the bathroom to wash up. Teresa turned to me and remarked "Mom, Matt said he didn't have anyone with him." At that very moment, an inaudible voice spoke to me: "You see Sharon, I love that boy as much as you do. I sent his angel to ride with him." Caught completely off guard, I couldn't make a reply. I was dumb-struck. What I had seen was a figure of a young man dressed in a plaid shirt with flowing, shoulder length hair. An Angel? Is that what a 70's angel looks like? After regaining my composure, I thanked God that he loved our only son, too.

Now, Matt was not perfect by any means. After all, neither of his parents had reached sainthood. He was never on drugs and told me once that "smoking stinks!" It displeased him when any of his friends asked to smoke in his car. He had tried both, but neither made an impression on this clean, well groomed youngster. Although he was not an alcoholic, he did take an occasional drink. Matt was happy, fun-loving and he never met a stranger. He had a way of making friends out of acquaintances. If you had met and talked with him for only a short time, he would have you feeling like you had known him for years.

Some of his choices of friends and activities greatly displeased both his father and I. We had committed him to God at birth and now we pleaded with God for guidance.

On Wednesday, August 24, both girls went with their father to prayer meeting. I stayed behind to have a "heart to heart" with our son.

After Matt showered, he came barefoot into the living room, dressed only in his jeans. He sat on the sofa. I began by telling him how unhappy we were with some of the choices he was making. I assured him that we both loved him dearly and only wanted his happiness and safety. I told him we just couldn't stand to see him being hurt without saying something.

God opened my mouth and I began to recall to Matt the familiar story of Jesus' death, the same story he had heard so many times at church, school and family worship for nineteen years. I explained that as Jesus hung on the cross, His Father couldn't bear to watch His Son being hurt either. He went so far as to draw a dark cloud around the cross so the world would not see the Father of the universe weep as His Son suffered in agony and shame and died alone for the sins of the world. Matt was visibly moved.

For the first time, I was able to recount to him the incident of the angel in his car and the words spoken to me. When I finished, I said "Matt, apparently God has something very special for you to do." With that, he looked at me with those moist blue eyes and said "Mom, I wish I knew what it was." I gave him a big hug and assured him that someday, we would know. He dressed and left to see his friends. I thanked God for giving me words to say and the roots of love for that boy grew deeper in my heart.

Three weeks later, on September 16, at 2:00 A. M., the phone rang. John turned on the light and reached for the phone.

"Hello."

"Are you Mr. Estrada?"

"Yes."

"Do you have a son, Matthew?"

"Yes."

"Does he own a red Pontiac Firebird?"

"Yes."

"Mr. Estrada, I am the coroner in Anderson, Alabama. Your son is dead."

John turned to me and said, "Matt is dead." "No" I screamed, jumping out of bed. "No! No! Who does that stranger on the phone think he is, telling us our son is dead? He doesn't even know Matt! What a cruel, heartless joke! Besides, that is not the way parents are supposed to be told."

I had often heard that a local policeman was dispatched to deliver such a message. As a minister, my husband had, on many occasions, been given the duty to inform parents of the death of a child or loved one. This is not how it was supposed to happen. I was angry. My husband was still talking to the man on the phone. I felt alone. I was scared. Our youngest daughter, Angela was asleep across the hall. Hearing my screams and sobs, she awoke.

"Mom, what's wrong?" she said through half-opened eyes.

"Matt's dead" I replied as we fell into each other's arms and wept.

It seemed like ages before John hung up the phone. He gave me the details he felt I could handle. We three wept, prayed and then called the academy girl's dean. Teresa must be told.

The dean woke the principal who joined her in the dean's apartment. Matt had been at the academy the previous year and was admired by the students and teachers, and the principal was no exception. He was admired and loved, not for his grades which were only slightly above passing, but for his winning smile and personality. Mr. Coy and Mrs. Hayes informed Teresa about her brother's death. After sun-up, the deans husband, a pilot, flew Teresa the 90 miles home.

When someone dies or is critically ill, the pastor is called. He immediately goes to the side of the family. But who does the pastor call when his family is in crisis? John and I looked at one another, then reached for the phone. John dialed our conference president and friend, Al McClure. By now, it was 5:00 A. M.

John spoke "Elder McClure."

"Yes, John" came the reply.

Then I blurted into the phone, "We need your help!" and I broke into sobs. My husband proceeded to explain that Matt had been killed in a car accident. He prayed with us and before 8:30, he and Conn Arnold were in our driveway to give us a hug and words of comfort. They had arranged for our larger family of minister friends to be notified. On Monday, they joined us and the family of the other young victim of the tragedy at the church while Conn Arnold led in a memorial service. Matt and his friend were buried side-by-side. At the cemetery, I knelt at the casket and said "Lord, I do not know, but I will not question why this had to happen." Through the years, that has been the hardest promise I have ever had to keep, although I have speculated from time to time as I see tragedies, war, drugs and violence. I thank God that He saw fit to spare our son those pains.

Matt's body was left at the cemetery and his red car, smashed again, was towed to the junk yard. This time, no one was there to claim it and resurrect it. Unlike the car, however, Matt awaits the call of the Redeemer to a new life without heartaches.

About a week before the accident, I had come in from work to see my son draped over the front end of his car. He was adjusting something under the hood. I asked him what he was doing and he informed me that he was tightening up the motor mounts broken in the previous accident. I peered under the hood and, for the first time, realized the enormous size of the engine. The engine alone looked as big as our small "economy car."

I recall saying "Well, there is no way that engine is going to come out of there." Little did I know the importance of the motor mounts. After the accident, a mechanic told us that unless the motor mounts are fastened securely, the engine itself could rear up like an airplane if the car reached a certain speed. Pressing the accelerator could cause the car to speed out of control, which is just what happened.

Small things like motor mounts, of which I knew little, could have saved two boys' lives. However, I did not know and therefore did not insist that they be corrected. Matt's compulsion for power and control was, in the end, the cause of his death.

Another compulsion that we noticed throughout his young lifetime was one to be neat and clean. He spent a lot of time in the shower. Every strand of his golden blond hair had its place. He had beautiful, very neat and legible handwriting. As a pre-teen, he never liked to get his hands dirty. He was a meticulous artist. The lines of his pen and pencil drawings were laid down with precision and deliberate strokes. Often, his dad and I wondered what he would do when he grew up. But with his love for motor cycles and cars, he reluctantly got black grease on his hands and under his finger nails.

His compulsion to own things became more evident to us after his death. I discovered a box of receipts he had saved and tags from clothing, electronics and car parts, his proof of ownership. In another box was every letter and card sent from his beloved, the mother of his baby daughter. These were evidence of his need for something to call his own.

Regretfully, I never spent the time with Matt that I should have after the birth of our daughters, especially the second one, when he had needed me most. I feel pain in my soul that cannot be soothed in this lifetime. In heaven, that boy and I have a lot of things to talk about.

It was April of 1992 before the memory of Matt's abuse hit me like icy cold water, when I realized what had happened to that little boy almost thirty-two years before.

On April 5th, as I drove from Nashville to Chattanooga on Sunday afternoon, a song on the radio triggered a memory that replayed the incident and the flow of tears wouldn't stop. I was alone. I realized the danger I was in on the interstate because I could not stop crying. God and I had quite a conversation. I said, "Lord, I can't see where I'm going. You will have to drive for me," at which time I put my white Reliant in "automatic pilot."

It was only then that I felt the answer to my unasked question of 12 years earlier: "Why? Why did Matt die?" There, with tear swollen eyes, a wad of tissues in one hand and the other on the steering wheel, I heard my Lord say to me, "Don't let another child of mine die with that hurt in his heart. Little boys must be told that sexual abuse is "not your fault!" It is never right for an older child or adult to take advantage of a young boy or girl.

Matt and I have much catching up to do in heaven. I must tell him how sorry I am that I didn't know how to help him with his pain. Then, I'll let him know how his young life gave me inspiration to write this book and to affirm other children, both girls and boys.

Only after his tragic death were my eyes opened to the pearl in my own home.

11

God On Trial

(Creator of Pearls)

"Where was God when I was being abused? Why didn't God answer my prayers for help? Where are the miracles today? Doesn't God hear me? How can I love or trust a God who would allow a child to be abused? Did I not matter to him? Wasn't He listening to my agonized screams for help? What kind of God is He anyway?"

These and many more questions have been asked by children and adults who have endured the pain and shame of child abuse. They are questions that are not easily answered, questions that can only be answered by God himself, questions that will only be answered in eternity. Who would presume to speak for God? Who can know the heart of God? No earthly human, that's for sure! Yet we try to explain the apparent absence of God to the doubting and hurting.

God is the Father of the universe, the Father of all mankind. A good father wants what is best for his offspring. Why is it then that God was so far away when children were being violated?

Before the world was created, a plan of redemption was designed. Should mankind disobey God's perfect order of things, there would be a back-up plan to put into motion immediately. The dreaded disobedience happened, breaking the heart of God.

Adam and Eve, perfect human creations, listened to Lucifer's lies: "God is not telling you the whole truth. Your eyes will be opened and you will be as Gods, yourselves, and you won't die." Listening to the voice of Lucifer caused them to doubt their loving Creator. They first entertained doubt, then temptation and finally, disobedience.

66

Immediately, the pair realized the mistake they had made and wished to undo their disobedience. The robe of light that God gave them for covering and warmth was gone. They hid themselves while they frantically picked large leaves and knitted them together with sticks and stems to cover their naked bodies. The story is found in Genesis.

When God called upon them that evening as was His routine, they were not eager to see Him. In fact, the couple hid themselves, afraid to answer as God walked through the garden calling to them. When at last they made an appearance, God asked "What is this that you have done?" When they told Him they had been deceived, God's heart was broken. The dreaded day had arrived after all. It was only to be a back-up plan, a last resort, not something He thought He would ever need. With everything so perfect, why would His creation want anything more? The unexpected had happened!

Except for the disobedience of these two people, the earth was perfect. God was disappointed that His creation was ruined. Like an artist who had in front of him a spoiled canvas, He could have discarded the whole scene and started over. Had He done just that, the tempter would have said, "You don't dare disobey God or He will destroy you. You can't have any mind of your own, make your own choices, or do your own thing because God is a tyrant who requires blind obedience."

Although God was grieved, He dared not wipe out Adam and Eve and start over. The back-up plan was put into action. This secondary plan called for someone else to die instead of Adam and Eve. God the Son had already volunteered for execution. Rather than Adam and Eve dying for their own sins, God the Son stepped into take their place. A stay of execution was issued for mankind. From that hour, free choice was granted. Lucifer, his followers, and the watching universe could not say that God was an unfair tyrant.

Because of man's disobedience, God the Son left the security of His heavenly home to become the sacrifice, four thousand years later. God the Father was grieved at the prospect of the loneliness of Heaven without His Son. Yet, they both had agreed it was the only way to save the fallen race.

Christ, the Son of God, became an innocent baby with a death sentence. He grew into a toddler, learning to walk and talk. He became an adolescent who sat at his mother's knee, learning about living on earth and the youth, working with His earthly father in the carpenter's shop fashioning furniture, bowls and doors from wood that He had spoken into existence. Chased, plotted against and abused throughout His life, He made the ultimate sacrifice of being hanged naked on rough hewn timbers just outside the city walls of Jerusalem, for all to witness.

The heartbreak of the Father was so great that He drew a dark cloud around the cross. Christ, alone in the darkness, cried out "My God, my God, why have You forsaken me?" God the Father, in His sadness could not bear to see His Son suffering. Putting a black cloud between Himself and the cross, God would not have to watch His Son suffer and die. The plan had been discussed and agreed upon four thousand years earlier. The Father was not to interfere. As bad as He wanted to, as hard as He fought with second thoughts, the Father kept his distance. He could have appeared and swept His Son up in His arms, but the plan would not be complete. Instead, the Father wept. Some say it rained that day. Were the raindrops the tears of the Heavenly Father? It broke his heart of love every time an innocent animal had to be sacrificed. It was only because of man's disobedience that this was necessary. For four thousand years, it was the practice to sacrifice animals for the sins of humanity. When Christ came to the earth to live and die, His sacrifice was the last one required. Since then, Christians have not been required or obligated to shed blood for sins.

Where was God when you were being abused? Why did He not come to rescue you? Why was no miracle performed to save you from the abuse? God was behind the dark cloud just as He was at Golgotha. When He did not come and rescue you, it was not because He couldn't. All power is His. If He used that power to rescue us every time we got into trouble, He would be accused of interfering with man's free choice. God did not take the fruit out of Eve's hand. She was given the same free choice that is extended to you and me. A miraculous rescue was not performed because

He would be accused of putting a "hedge" around His people and never allowing them to suffer, but always to prosper. Read the story of Job in the book by the same name in the Holy Bible.

During their recovery, some victims of abuse have asked the question: "Where was God when I was being abused?" Judy asked the same thing. Later in her recovery process, she was shown a weeping Jesus sitting on the foot of the bed.

> "I remembered laying, torn and bleeding on the bed, begging Jesus to save me from further pain, but it seemed as though my words bounced back at me from the ceiling. I felt totally alone and helpless, and cried 'Why, God? How could you let this happen the day after my baptism?'
>
> Thirty years later, I finally received an answer to my question. As I recalled the incident, I seemed to see another person in the room, sitting on the side of the bed. I knew instantly that it was Jesus. As I lay crying, His tears mingled with my own. When my abuser came back to beat and rape me again, Jesus held me in His arms and gave me the strength to survive. When I wanted to die, He showed me the nail prints in His hands and feet, and finally, I understood.
>
> He also had to suffer the results of sin. He knew what I was going through and it hurt Him too. He didn't want any of His children to suffer, but when He gave man the freedom of choice, some chose the wrong path, and the innocent sometimes suffered. He suffered because of man's sins, but when He gained the victory on the cross, He gained it for each one who accepts Him as their Savior. But my abuser was so controlled by sin that he could no longer hear God's pleading. All Jesus could do was give me the strength to endure and stay close by my side. But someday, He will take me home to live with Him, where no pain or suffering will ever again exist."

God does not want any of His children to suffer, yet children suffer every day. Why? I read a quote once that said, "God could not be everywhere so He made mothers." There is a certain amount of truth in that statement. At times, mothers seem to see everything, be everywhere and know everything. It is true that God made parents and gave to them the responsibility of raising and nurturing their offspring.

It is the parents' responsibility to feed their children so they will grow into adulthood and have children of their own. It is the parents' responsibility to clothe their children, protecting them from the elements and the shame of nakedness. It is the parents' responsibility to teach their children what is right, honest and good, to set boundaries for physical and emotional safety. It is the parents' responsibility to provide a safe environment for their children, a home with warmth and unselfishness. It is the parents' responsibility to nurture their children.

Virginia Satir said once that we need at least six hugs per day in order to feel loved. Most parents fail here. Some parents are proud of themselves when they spend 45 seconds of "quality time" with their youngster.

The Heavenly Father is more than willing to provide all these things, but He gave this responsibility to parents. Unfortunately, many parents, because of their own selfish desires, are miserable substitutes. Were it not for unselfish parents who would rather die themselves than have one of their little ones suffer, humanity would have destroyed itself before now.

Bring to mind, if you can, the *best* person that you have ever met. Then imagine someone who is one hundred times *better,* and you will begin to know how much God loves you. This God *did* die for his children.

A child is not for hurting; any child, any where, any time. Children are to be loved and protected. The earthly parent is to take on that responsibility every time sexual intercourse leads to conception.

Because of the sinful heart, some parents are selfish. Thinking only of themselves and their wants, not needs, they allow their innocent children to be violated. They then have failed their commission as parents.

When parents, who are to serve in the place of the Heavenly Father, fail to provide safety for their children, God is blamed. He is accused of not caring. He is indicted for being negligent. His reputation is slandered and His own character is questioned.

Often, we hear Eve being blamed for the sin and heartaches of the world. But if we had been the one under the shadow of the tree, would we have done a better job of resisting the serpent's temptation?

Blame should be put where it truly belongs: selfish parents and ultimately, the father of lies, Satan himself. The lie he told Adam and Eve, "You will be as gods yourself," is the root of selfishness. "You can have it all. You can do anything you want, no matter who you hurt. If it feels good, do it. Live for today. Take, take, take. . ." The forces of evil are fighting against good and God is being blamed for all the evil, while Satan smiles. The finger is being pointed at God and doubts are raised about His character to the delight of Satan. He is free then to do more of the same, spreading doubt and suspicion about the Model Parent.

Victims then are sure that God does not care or He would rescue them. Victims of child abuse find it hard to believe and trust God.

After reading this chapter, I hope you will better see who is to blame for your pain. Here is how I answered this question in a letter to a young person who could not love or trust God:

Dear Cara:

I understand that your abuser used God as a cover-up and a battering ram to hurt you. He was not man enough himself to take the responsibility for his own actions, but used God to excuse his own selfish desires.

To illustrate, let's say you were driving down Broad Street in your town and were hit by a red Ford pick-up truck. The accident demolished your car, left you with a broken leg, your shoulder out of socket, and a concussion. Who is to blame for your suffering? Who is responsible for the months that you must spend in therapy to learn to walk again? Who was it that caused you to bleed, and every

71

muscle to cry out in excruciating pain? Was the red Ford pick-up truck responsible? You are right. It was the <u>driver</u> of the truck whom you take to court to pay for the medical and hospital bills, replacement of your car, and lost wages.

You see Cara, it wasn't God who broke the little girl into pieces, but an abuser who was not man enough to take the blame for his own actions.

Where was God when this was happening? When you cried, He cried! When you screamed, He screamed! You were His child being abused and what was done to you was done to Him! He felt your pain and loves you without condition. The abuse was not your fault, neither was it God's fault. The red Ford pick-up truck was not to blame for the devastation the driver caused you. It is the driver who has to pay for the damages. Your abuser was the driver, and he alone caused the heartache.

Believe it or not, BAD THINGS DO HAPPEN TO GOOD PEOPLE! The devil, not God is the architect of all the suffering that humanity has had to endure.

God is love! He makes the sun rise and set. He makes the flowers bloom and the birds sing. He put love in the little baby's eyes and He would never take it away.

Sincerely,
Sharon

Recently a friend said "If God shielded us from the devil all the time, we would never know how bad he is!" How true that is! Because we meet him face to face, we see him for who he really is: an evil, vile and destructive adversary. Lucifer's purpose in the beginning was to cast doubt on God's character. Through the years, his followers still distort God's reputation. There is nothing that he fears as much as that we shall become acquainted with God.

Where is God when it hurts? He is the same place he was when His own Son was hanging on the cross: behind the clouds, weeping. His loving hands shape perfect pearls, hidden in lives of pain. I do not presume to speak for God, but this is how I see Him. I trust it will explain some of your doubts, too.

72

12

Sand And Pearls

As the grain of sand enters, the oyster immediately notices the sharp foreign object. Its tender body is irritated and scratched. The Creator put instinct inside the small animal to promote healing. It covers the irritating object with layer upon layer of the same type of material the inside of its shell is lined with. In time, it is less irritating.

Victims feel the pain caused by the foreign object of abuse. Many "clam up" in their "shells" and hide because of the hurt and embarrassment. Their shells may be isolation, busyness, phobias, compulsions, etc. By hurting in silence, they cover the irritant with their own being. Body stressors deter growth, inflict physical pain, and encourage disease by the breakdown of the immune system. What happens to the physical body while it tries to keep the emotional body undetected is not realized many times until physical forces are depleted. Ulcers, insomnia, migraines, and arthritis are some of the first symptoms of repressed abuse. Often the body is physically and emotionally bankrupt before a victim will seek help.

A psychologist friend told me, "Sharon, I used to ask my clients about incest and sexual abuse on about the fifth visit. Now I ask them the first time they come to my office. This practice has helped me to diagnose and start treatment sooner." As more and more people are honest with themselves and speak out, we see many symptoms in common: Promiscuousness, low self-esteem, eating disorders, and drug and alcohol abuse are very recognizable symptoms of a childhood gone wrong.

To begin the healing process, you must face the hurt, admit it happened. It really is O.K. to say "It happened to me. But it was not my fault!"

Now it is time to process the pain, give back the shame. Working through past issues is a necessary part of the recovery. Many victims ask themselves, "Why can't I just forget it? No one has to know. They will blame me if I tell now!"

It is possible to block many things from the conscious mind, but the body still remembers. Delayed reactions to certain stimuli will "tell on you," even if you try to hide it. Compulsive behaviors and habits are ways the body lets us know it still remembers the wrongs. The sooner we listen to ourselves, the sooner recovery will take place. A review of the incidents will validate us. As we recall our age and size, we realize there is no way that a child that age and size could imagine these things.

Write out the details of the abuse and how you reacted:

- ---- Were you able to cry about the hurt?
- ---- Did you get angry?
- ---- Did you feel it was your fault?
- ---- Were you threatened if you told?
- ---- Did the abuser tell you that you were responsible?
- ---- Did you withdraw from friends and family because of guilt?
- ---- Did you feel embarrassed?
- ---- Did you feel rejected and betrayed?
- ---- Did you dissociate yourself from the incident and pretend it was not happening to you?
- ---- In your memory, were you looking on as an observer?
- ---- Did you feel betrayed by your own body because it responded to the stimulation?
- ---- Can you grieve now for the small, helpless child you were?
- ---- Can you now find any good in what happened then?
- ---- Can you see how your life was influenced, shaded and clouded by just one incident?
- ---- If you were rewriting your life story, what would you insert in place of the abuse? Create a happy memory and ending for the little child.
- ---- What do you wish your parents, teachers or guardians had taught you so you could have told sooner? And how could you have been able to stand up for yourself and say no?

You are on your way to recovery, one step at a time. It is a process, a **grieving process!** Recovery involves feeling the grief over your lost childhood; it means facing issues of abandonment and broken trust. Questions of "why" must be confronted. By reading this book, you are taking at least one step: knowledge about abuse. Now, let's find that beautiful pearl!

The following is a prayer offered before a VOHC Support Group meeting:

Heavenly Father,

We really don't know what a father is. We have not had good examples. We thought a father was supposed to take care of his kids, but we have been hurt by ours. We've felt pain, loneliness and fear.

We depend now on you to give us love, comfort and protection. Show us that you care about us. We have been hiding for many years, suffering shame and pain. We felt that we were ugly, dumb, stupid and to blame for the bad things that happened to us. We trust you to get us out of this mess we are in. You told us in your word that you love us. We are counting on that.

We also know you love the ones who hurt us. Help us to forgive them. You sent your only Son, Jesus, to die for them too. And if you can die and forgive them, then we can forgive with your help.

Show us your love. Give us strength and the comfort of your presence. Help us in this quietness to hear your whispers of peace.

We give you Lord, the sacrifice of our lives, small and pitiful offerings that we are. We present them to you for cleansing, remaking and refilling.

We beg you to care for our little ones. We are scared for them to go out in the world each day. Place a hedge of angels about our children. Shield them from the angry adversary who delights in the pain of children and the destruction of families. We do not want him to have the victory. We love and trust you with our lives and recovery. Thank you for hearing and answering our petitions; Amen.

You Speak Of Love
by Heather

You speak of `love,' well I'll tell you friend,
I've been promised `Love' again and again.
Love that flamed ever so brightly,
Love that laughed ever so lightly.

Love so fertile, it made itself grow-
but now it's gone, and where is the glow?
What is left of the love that I'd known?
Nothing but a cold, lonely and hardened stone.

I am a stone of the hardest making -
A stone with no heart for your breaking,
A stone that feels no pain and hurts.
Why waste emotions to be treated like dirt?

I am a stone of the hardest making -
A stone that has no threat of breaking . . .
A stone that doesn't mess with a love that lies . . .
A stone feels no pain and it never, ever cries!

13

Pain And Pearls

It is time to give the responsibility for the abuse to the right person or persons. At the time of the abuse, the offender made you feel at fault. You have carried that guilt. It is heavy. It can and will weigh you down. You may have carried that guilt and shame for years, even decades. The saddest part is that it never did belong to you! Your abusers did a good "sales job." You bought it, you believed it and all the time, it was a lie!

As a child, you were probably taught to respect older people; parents, teachers, coaches, pastors, scout leaders, etc. What they said must be true, so you believed them, even if it didn't make sense. You reasoned, "If it is O.K., fun or good, why is it a secret?" Good was bad, bad was good; right was wrong, wrong was right! You became confused and doubted your own belief system. One young person told me, "One minute I knew something was right and the next minute, I didn't know anything."

The first thing I tell clients who come to see me is "Remember! It was not your fault!" Then I have them tell me, "It was not my fault." Again and the third time, "Say it like you really believe it!" Their ears must hear their own mouth tell them "It was not my fault!" That one step will cause the burden they have carried to be no more. It is not their fault or their shame.

Jesus once spoke to his friends and disciples, saying "There is nothing concealed that will not be disclosed, or hidden that will not be made known. What you have said in the dark will be heard in the daylight, and what you have whispered in the ear in the inner rooms will be proclaimed from the roofs," Luke 12:2-3, New International Version.

Yes, the abuse will be spoken aloud. Scripture also says, "Be sure your sins will find you out." A clearer meaning is: *You can be sure your sins will find you out.* The abuse and abusers will be in the newspapers, on the television news and talk-shows, and talked about at the barber shop and the market. Nothing needs to be secret anymore! You have permission to give back the guilt to the right person. It is not only your right but your responsibility! If your abuse is left hidden, other children may be injured by the same offender. It is your privilege to stop the cycle by naming the accused. Then and only then will he or she get necessary psychological help and spiritual healing.

When confronting an abuser, I never ask a yes or no question. You already know they did it. So I never give them the opportunity to deny it. DENIAL IS THE EXPECTED RESPONSE! You can count on it! What I do ask is "How old were you when you were abused?" The answer most of the time tells me the age of their first victim. Also, because the emotional growth is stunted the instant the sexual abuse takes place, the abuser will relate to the same age or size child as he was when first abused.

How do you give back the blame? You may confront the abuser directly, in person or you may do it in a letter, mailed or unmailed, or you may do it verbally to an empty chair. If he or she is no longer alive, you could make a trip to the cemetery and verbally leave the years of pain they caused you. However you choose to do it, remember you are an adult now. No longer are you a small, defenseless child! You can speak as an adult. Do not accept denial! You know it happened, he knows he did it, God knows he did it, and heaven has recorded it!

The bruise caused by the sand can now begin to heal. You will feel the pain over and over again, but time will heal. One thing time cannot do though, is erase the scars. The scars are a part of you and they can become your strength if you let them. Remember, everything that has happened to you influences you for a lifetime. The decisions or choices you make are colored by the experiences and influences of your backgrounds.

You will make mistakes, but God can and will help you and use you if you let Him. He says, "I will **NEVER** leave thee or forsake thee." No matter how bad you feel about your past, God will only see a perfect child. How is this possible? Christ stands between you and God the Father. When the Father looks at you, He sees *you* through the perfect life and sacrifice of Jesus. Because Jesus too was a victim of physical and verbal abuse, He is the most Precious Pearl of all ages.

14

Ritual Abuse

(Baroque Pearls)

On display at the Pearl Factory was a strand of exquisite but oddly shaped gems. "What are those?" I inquired. "Baroque pearls," came the reply. Immediately, I understood how they came to be called Baroque pearls, different yet beautiful! An odd shaped irritant had entered the shell, and oysters, doing what oysters do best, took what they were given and made pearls. Though they were odd or perhaps teardrop shaped, they were no less a thing of beauty. Strung together with like variations, they were splendid to behold. The color was a soft off-white, almost gray, with all the iridescent beauty given them by the Creator. Rejected at first because their shape was not perfectly round, the baroque pearls possessed a beauty all their own when combined with others like them. I could only dream of a treasure like this! However, now I am finding baroque pearls of a different kind.

My telephone rings at almost any time, day or night. On the other end of the line may be someone from the other side of the United States. "Sharon, you don't know me but I got your name from a friend of mine back east. She said I needed to talk to you." As she continues, another horrendous story emerges and I pray silently, "God, give me the words and the wisdom to meet this need." Sometimes, it is a grandmother in tears about her grandchildren who have been abused. Often, it is a middle-aged woman who shares her own painful childhood. It may be a father with concerns about his son living with a new step-dad with a history of gay living before marrying the child's mother. Sometimes, it is a young person wanting to know if the pain will go away if she just doesn't tell anybody and does not confront her abuser.

Until the summer of 1992, I thought I had heard all the stories of abuse that could be told. Little did I know that multiple personalities and Satanic ritual abuse were about to become my next lessons. Baroque pearls had been created. These pearls evolved when the worst form of irritant, Satanic Ritual Abuse (SRA) was forced upon them as children and adults. Physically tortured beyond belief and terrified into silence, these pearls became the odd ones in our society. Hiding a secret that no one else knew, they didn't seem to fit in anywhere. But oh, what a thing of beauty when lifted by the hand of a loving Creator-Artist from their painful past!

From many miles away, over the phone came the quiet voice of Rachel. "Sharon, I have this terrible feeling that a memory is coming back and I am so afraid. You are the only one I know and trust, who can ask me the right questions."

"Rachel," I said, "You are too far away for me to help you safely. If you remember a terrible experience, you should not be alone. Talk to your therapist and see if you can spend a week or so in the hospital. You need to be in a safe place." The next time she called me, it was from a hospital psychiatric ward. Through a series of group and drawing therapies, Satanic Ritual Abuse began to emerge from her memories.

Another time, Linda spoke to me. Her abuse was many years in duration. Her abusers were dead. Still, some memories refused to be released from her subconscious until months later. Again, Satanic ritual abuse came to light.

Gean told me much the same story. My heart felt like bleeding for the little girls and boys I was hearing about.

For anyone unacquainted with Satanic Ritual Abuse, please believe me when I tell you, it is real! "We wrestle not against flesh and blood, but against powers, against the rulers of the darkness of this world . . . Ephesians 6:12 Satan works in darkness and blackness.

When I was in high school, in an advanced home economics class, the teacher asked us to describe the color white and the color black. I thought that was a ridiculous assignment. Black

81

was black and white was white. After all, anyone could see that! Mrs. Stevens went on to explain. "Black is made up of all the colors of the rainbow in the *absence of light*. White, on the other hand, is made of all the colors of the rainbow in the *presence of light*." Since color can only be seen in light, it started to make sense. Blue socks and red socks were really just black socks until I turned on the light and could distinguish between the colors. It took the presence of light to reveal the truth.

Satan works his evil deeds in darkness and causes his followers to do evil deeds under a cover of darkness as well. Billie drew black Birthday cakes with black candles. While doing some memory work with me, she recalled chocolate birthday cakes throughout her childhood. What caused them to be black in her memory was that they were part of a November ritual celebration each year at the park. The cover of darkness caused them to appear black.

It never entered my mind that evil forces would shatter the lives of so many children in Christian homes. You may think, "surely they are protected from such evil." Only to a point. We, as humans, fail to entreat the Holy Spirit on behalf of our children. "You have not, because you ask not," James 4:2. Parents should plead with the Lord each morning for the protection of their little ones. Our children then should be taught that evil exists and what they should do when confronted with it.

What emerged from the people I talked with were similar stories with a familiar ring. Again and again, it was the same story and the same pain with different faces and different places. Some common themes included:

Bad odors, bad taste, strange drink
Basements, dungeons, caves, pits, being buried alive
Black cats, panthers, black dogs, or white kittens
Black Mass, Black Sabbath, Friday the 13th, Halloween
Black robes, dark drapes
Blood, dead bodies, caskets
Candles, chains, claws, pentagrams, circles, chants

Cold, damp, dark
Dead babies, men, women, and animals
Demons, evil spirits
Drugs, hallucinations
Goats, rabbits, snakes, spiders and bugs
Hypodermic needles, knives and daggers
Left handed leaders, secret organizations
Little girls, little boys
Missing time, bad feelings
Naked bodies
Rape, sodomy
Upside-down crosses, altars, red roses, black roses, and
    the list goes on and on . . .

As these men and women began to unfold their stories, it was clear to see what had taken place even thirty to forty years before. Satan, knowing he has but a short time, "Walketh about like a roaring lion, seeking whom he may devour," I Peter 5:8.

Satan is not worried about the congregation of evil-doers in his ranks. But the saints in the church are a different story. If he can destroy the families of these church-going saints, he can smell victory. It is with this in mind that he reaches into the homes of Christians, often strict and over-zealous church-goers, and no one will suspect.

Personalities are changed. Unsuspecting friends, family, neighbors and church associates are none the wiser. When Satan controls an individual, they will do things they never intended, and may not remember for decades.

Not all men and women who remember incidents of Satanic Ritual Abuse grew up in so-called Christian homes. Some turned to Christianity in later life in search of the peace they had never before known.

But often, one or both parents "had a form of godliness," yet used their own children in satanic rituals. These parents were sometimes elders, teachers, deacons or preachers. They told the children that they were evil and bad, and God did not love them.

To the rest of the congregation, these were righteous and trusted individuals. The only ones who knew the truth were the children, who were scared into silence.

Even if a child is brave enough to talk, he or she is disbelieved. Leaders of these cults know that the more bizarre the rituals, the less anyone will be apt to believe it could really happen. Victims are put down as having vivid imaginations.

Evil forces are as real in the 20th century as they were when Christ walked the earth. The evil spirits He cast out of the naked man living in the cemetery were legions, or a mob. There were so many that they drove a herd of 2000 pigs to their death in the Sea of Galilee, Mark 5:1-16.

Let's not fool ourselves into believing that things like that only happened while our Lord walked on the earth. Evil angels were on the earth before Christ came and are here yet, today. After the war in heaven, one third of all the created angels were thrown out of heaven to the earth. Christ came to destroy the power of sin. Because of His death, we can claim eternal life. But Satan and his angels are with us today in every form of disguise. We may not recognize them, but "their work is only evil continually," Genesis 6:5. We may have the power over sin and evil as a free gift, simply for the asking. "Call upon me and I will answer," Jeremiah 33:3.

For everything in Christianity, Satan has a counterfeit. Satan copies, changes, mocks, perverts or reverses every ceremony, ordinance or symbol:

---- The Cross of Christ --- Satan turns it upside-down.

---- The five-pointed star is reversed and the head of a wolf or goat is imposed over it, making the pentagram.

---- The communion cup with the symbolic blood of Christ represented by pure grape juice is mocked by the use of actual blood from sacrificed babies, adults or animals, often mixed with urine and drugs.

---- Unleavened bread, representing the flesh of Christ, is mocked by the consumption of actual flesh of the sacrifices already mentioned.

---- A sacrificial altar, often of stone, is fashioned to replace the communion table which holds the precious and sacred emblems of Christ's body and blood.

---- The Christian rite of marriage is mocked by dressing a young girl in a white dress. An animal is sacrificed. The blood is then smeared on her chest after her dress is split down the front. She is given blood to drink and is raped in a "wedding night" ritual.

Baroque pearls have been through the worst kind of abuse. Real beauties like these have had unique experiences that can only make them stronger as they allow God to heal their pain. The good news is that baroque pearls are magnificent and strong! They have looked evil in the face and have been redeemed by the Pearl of Great Price.

15

Multiple Personality Disorder

(Shattered Pearls)

Some of the most intelligent humans have become shattered pearls! The irritants came rapidly and brutally. Unbearable trauma, torture and abuse have caused these pearls to fracture. More than once, and often through decades of abuse, these pearls split as new traumas accosted them. These fractured pearls are known as multiples.

Multiple Personality Disorder (MPD), or Dissociative Disorders (DD) have been recognized in recent years as a valid mechanism to cope or escape in the face of horrific trauma or violent accidents. It is in no way a sign of insanity or weakness. In fact, the opposite is true. To remain sane, a child or adult will block the horrible memories of physical or emotional pain in order to cope with reality. MPD is common in victims of extreme physical and sexual abuse, especially if associated with satanic rituals. In general, the public does not understand how a person could have more than one personality. How the personalities came about in the first place is an even greater mystery.

To have lived through some of the abuses is nothing short of a miracle. The only way some have made it at all is by splitting or fragmenting. Psychiatrists say it takes a strong and intelligent person to fragment. Let me explain, as I understand it, so you can get a feel for this mystery.

If, during a particularly violent incident of abuse or trauma, the "host" or real person (most often a young child) cannot cope with the emotional or physical pain, they will unconsciously delegate the memory to an alternative (alter) personality. That personality is in charge of that incident and the host person does not have to deal with it, even to the point of forgetting it ever happened. It is then stored immediately in the long-term memory of the brain, not to be dealt with until a safer time. This is why it is a protecting or coping mechanism, in that it preserves the sanity.

The more violently abusive the incidents the host personality has had to endure, the more alter personalities are created. Each has its own secret, painful event or types of events to guard with all the emotions related to each. For example, a particularly violent episode of abuse may carry with it so much physical or emotional pain that the child or host personality may feel extreme hatred or rage. The child cannot deal with it because:

1) They *do not know how;*
2) It was so painful that they *do not want to remember;*
3) The child was drugged and they *cannot remember;*
      or
4) They were threatened with death so they *must not remember.*

More and more fragments or other personalities are needed to help preserve the sanity of the host person who has lived a lifetime of abuse.

Everything that has ever happened to us, everything we have heard or seen, is stored, and sometimes locked in the long-term memory of our brain. How are these memories retrieved? With a key! When the physical body is strong enough and the mind has the knowledge and education through years of training and experience, it will be safe to deal with the stored or locked pages of memory.

Usually, each personality has a name, and because of the age of the victim at the time of the incident, the personality may lock on to that age. For example, Sally may be the one that is flirty and Pete may be an angry one. The name may even reveal the feeling or emotion.

The gender of the personality does not necessarily reflect the gender of the host person. If, for example, a young girl is raped by a rough and burley aggressor, she may think to herself, "If I were a strong boy, this would not be happening to me." A strong boy's personality is called on to handle this pain and fight off the attacker. He may become very angry and even take on a deeper male-like voice. The incident is turned over to him and the memory blocked or filed away. When he is needed, his strong fighting nature comes back to defend the host in similar situations.

Subconsciously, these personalities may, on occasion, show themselves in unexplained anger, crying or flirtation. Only during the recovery process will they be recognized as another personality. Each will reappear in its own time, as a particular emotion is explored. The memory of the incident responsible for the creation of the alter personality will have to be dealt with now, as an adult.

All the physical and emotional pain is brought back and experienced again. Whereas the child was unable to handle the pain, it is now felt in the adult body surrounded by all the emotions of the incident.

What are the keys that unlock these personalities from their prison? The keys are sometimes called "triggers." A trigger can be the *smell* of the damp forest floor or the *sight* of a knife display in the mall. Sometimes, *seeing another child* who reminds them of themselves at a certain age or *wearing a particular article of clothing* can trigger a memory of something in the past. At first, he or she may ask what it has to do with anything in the present. The answer may be the beginning of uncovering traumatic experiences from the past. Memories begin flooding back, and a trigger or key is determined.

Do these personalities reveal themselves to anyone else? Yes. Often, a personality will converse with someone they trust, such as a close friend or a therapist, without the host person knowing about it. The host may refer to "lost time", time they cannot account for. It may be a time when an alter was in charge or active.

Alter personalities have called and talked with me on the telephone. They may identify themselves. Sometimes the only clue is a childlike voice or an accent. I've asked their age and other questions to help me establish that they are truly an alter personality and not the host person playing a trick. I may ask if the host personality knows they are calling. The answer is sometimes "No." Occasionally, we just have a friendly chat. Once I did something that provoked a feeling of gratitude, and the alter personality called to thank me. Sometimes, however, the alter personality may "tell on" the host person for something he or she has done or is about to do, such as feeling depressed, upset with someone, or contemplating suicide.

For example, on one occasion an alter personality, Brady, called to tell me that Heather had taken an overdose of her medication. I called the paramedics and raced to meet her at the hospital. As I kept vigil in the emergency room, nurses, technicians and doctors pumped Heather's stomach, took blood tests and forced liquid charcoal into her stomach. I stood by her hospital bed. After I had prayed and waited many hours, Heather looked at me with fire in her eyes and questioned, "Why didn't you let me die?"

"Brady thought you needed help and called me," I said. Although it was her voice, she did not remember talking to me. Of the many personalities living or hiding in Heather, several learned to trust me enough to talk. Heather had 39 known personalities.

Because of her tortured past and her poor physical health caused by years of childhood abuse, six months after the episode in the emergency room, Heather was successful at committing suicide.

I ask, "Why did you have to leave? Heather, there were so many questions. You were a great teacher. I learned so much about abuse, MPD and love from you. But you died after the tenth try. No child should have had to endure your pain." A psychologist friend said to me once, "You can't help them. They will **all** eventually kill themselves." I hated that he offered no hope.

At the time I made Heather's acquaintance, I had no knowledge of how to help her. My hands were tied by lack of understanding. I didn't know what to do. Frankly, at that point, I'm not sure that I believed it was real. Like many others, I thought it was mental illness, an excuse for attention, demon possession, a weakness, sin, or denial of reality. I thought, "You poor thing. When you are converted, you won't have to play this game any more. You'll be normal (whatever that is) like the rest of us."

Now, years later, I wish I could have a second chance. I am confident that Heather would be alive if only I had known then what I know now.

When I began VOHC, Heather gave me a poem for the first brochure. One time, she handed me four different poems. Each was in a different and distinctive handwriting; each written by a different personality; each dripping with pain.

Many "horrific" episodes in the life of a child can cause so much physical and emotional pain that an alter personality is needed to help deal with reality. Jeanine had fractured into 27 different personalities. Once, while on her way to college, she found herself on the swings at a playground instead. Hours had passed and she did not recall how she had gotten there. She did not go to classes that day. Her books lay untouched on the car seat. Because of her many absences, she was forced to drop all classes. This same type of behavior also made it impossible to hold a job. She was declared mentally and physically disabled, and was approved for Supplemental Security Income.

Not all multiples are this noticeable. Many hold down jobs in the public for years. Others interact socially, shoulder to shoulder, without detection. Quite often, these people are not aware that they have MPD. It is possible to function productively in some environments without an episode of personality change.

Jeanine's psychologist had diagnosed the MPD, but offered little hope for recovery. In therapy, Jeanine realized that not only was her father an abuser but her mother, as well. Since her mother was a practicing Christian, she found it hard to accept her being a child abuser. She recalled many times when she was chased by her mother and whipped with a belt. The physical abuse was only part of the abusive treatment from her mother. Little Jeanine was taught about a "God of wrath and fear." She prayed often out of fear instead of love. As an adult, Jeanine learned to know the "God of Love" and knew the truth of His comfort in an hour of despair. She says, "I feel His love and I know he understands me so much more than I understand myself. It is He who sent some wonderful people into my life to help."

90

She remembered some of the painful things her parents did to her, but there were many blank spots. She remembered when the pain was so bad that she wanted to pass out. Later, she realized it was on those occasions that other personalities were being formed. She said, "No child could mentally survive the things I do remember, and I am well aware that there are many things I do not recall."

These children take longer to grow up emotionally. Physically, they look the same, but an inner turmoil may be manifested in sudden outbursts of anger, uncontrolled behavior, and physical symptoms of disease.

Persons with MPD may suffer an assortment of physical ailments. Their medicine cabinets may be bulging with prescriptions ordered by well-meaning but exasperated physicians. Not recognizing an alter personality with bizarre complaints or ailments, he may well prescribe still another antidepressant or pain medication. When the patient gets home with the medication, it may not alleviate the pain or agitation. Medications prescribed for one personality quite often do not help another. Add to that the fact that this patient may go to many doctors or specialists for various real or phantom illnesses or symptoms which their bodies display, and over medication is a very real possibility! Still another reason that some medications may not work is the fact that they have built up in immunity to many drugs because of years of ritual abuse. Ritual abuse is always accompanied by forced drug use, both prescription and street drugs.

Recently, I entered the hospital for a simple day-surgery procedure. The anesthetist told me before he put me to sleep that he would be using a drug that would make me so relaxed, I would be asleep, would feel no pain, and would not remember what was done to me. Sure enough, within an hour, I was awake and even if my life depended upon it, I could not tell you what they did to me. Only because the doctor told me can I describe the procedure.

After my short stay in day-surgery, I can honestly tell you "I remember nothing." In cult rituals, these same types of drugs are used on children and adults. Their bodies are used and abused, but they remember nothing! They remember nothing of the abuse, where they were taken, or how much time passed. Because these occurrences are repeated often, year after year, an immunity is built up in their bodies of which they are unaware.

Annie had gone to the doctor for a checkup because she was feeling weak, with pains in her joints. After a thorough examination, the doctor asked her if she had undergone a lot of surgeries. She assured him that she had not. Then the doctor informed her that her bones were that of an eighty-plus year old woman. He said her bones had aged even though she had not seen her 43rd birthday. This type of aging of the bones was usually caused by anesthesia. Annie had been a victim of childhood sexual and Satanic Ritual Abuse.

MPD is not a play for attention but an unconscious effort to stay alive. Some of these patients have suffered very real and disabling physical abuse. Scars, including vaginal and rectal tearing, can cause nerve damage and painful symptoms in later life. Until these persons come in touch with reality again and regain control over their lives, it is necessary for us to be very compassionate. Most of the time, you will never know a person, even a close friend or associate, has MPD. As stated before, these are highly intelligent persons, clever enough to create help for themselves as children and the personalities are even more clever to hide from their close friends and family.

My second encounter with MPD was Alissa. In the meantime, after Heather's death, I had been given a business card of a therapist who specialized in Dissociative Disorders, so I passed it on to her.

However, the next time, God did not let me off so easily. Rosie, who lived 700 miles away, was the worst case of SRA/MPD that I had ever heard of or even read about. In desperation, I cried, "O.K. God, You've convinced me that it is real! Now, what do I do about it?"

Since the disastrous experience with Heather, I had researched why it happens and learned much. But now, the question was "How do I help these people?" In each new situation, when I didn't know what to do, I would plead with the Heavenly

Father. "Lord, I need your help again. You have never let me down. I only want to be used by You and for Your Glory. I have other things I would like to do, God. You know I have lots of reading to catch up on and the craft cabinet in my bedroom is running over with projects that I would enjoy. But since you have called me to do this work for you, I'll wait to do the quiet things later." Always, as I prayed with my hands outstretched, God filled them. He had been faithful in the past and I had no reason to think He would let me down now.

As I was reading Dr. Ed Murphy's book, "A Handbook for Spiritual Warfare," I came upon a quote that made me think. On page 481, I read "In a traumatic experience in childhood or elsewhere along the way, a part of the person is split off and left behind. It is sealed off, somehow, by Satan. The personality that is split off remains *at that place, at that age*. Usually, this segment is **kept in darkness about Christ** or is held in the grip of some problem." (Italics provided)

"That's it!" I said out loud. "Those little personalities were kept in darkness about a loving Savior. The personalities are not other persons, only parts of the host person. Therefore, when the person or host may have come to know Christ, the personalities may still have been in hiding and were not introduced to Jesus at that time. Now that the host is physically and emotionally stronger, the personalities are agreeable to relinquish their hidden secrets.

It is altogether possible that young alters have not heard of the name or love of Jesus. Because of the fear attached to incidents, the alters may have hidden so deeply inside the subconscious that the name of Jesus did not reach them. As they find someone to trust again, they will emerge with their secrets.

The first hint of memory recall may be "flashbacks." Flashbacks are like still photos, freeze-framed. These pictures may seem strange, even scary at first. They may contain only portions of a repressed memory. In therapy, the rest of the memory may emerge along with an understanding of how it came to be locked away in the first place.

It is important to note here that not all persons with repressed memories have other personalities. But all multiple personalities do hold repressed memories belonging to the host. As they relinquish the memories, the host once again has that knowledge. It is then no longer necessary to be separate. Their work (hiding the painful memory) is over and they are free. As they learn to trust Jesus as the host does, they can share in the love, peace and joy of a Savior. When they ask Jesus to take away the pain, anger and fear and fill the void with His love, peace and joy, He comes in, bringing completeness and peace. It is not necessary for all repressed memories to be recalled. Only enough of the forgotten past is necessary for the host person to have an affirmation or validation that what they are seeing and feeling is real. The frustration is that they are often doubted, disbelieved, looked down on as outcasts, or viewed as demon possessed.

They are not possessed with demons! An evil Spirit must be invited in to possess its victim. Young victims are unwilling participants used by adult perpetrators. During the rituals, they may be told "You are evil, you belong to Satan." Being innocent, they unconsciously believe what they are told. Through this programming they are convinced that they are bad and evil. Some of the personalities may show some stubborn, angry, or even hateful actions but all are not necessarily demon possessed. A part of the victim must be willing to be possessed. Satan cannot truly possess a heart that is warmed by Christ and truly wants to live for him. Satan does not give up without a struggle though!

There are several ways to invite evil possession. Many of the toys and games that parents unwittingly buy for their children to play with have demons attached to them when they are manufactured. Dr. Murphy in *The Handbook for Spiritual Warfare* affirms this. Loose talk, including swearing and foul language are also the inventions of Satan. Questionable music and entertainment are other ways that invite Satan and demons into the home and heart.

The torturing of children until they "split" is the goal of the cult. They know when this split has occurred by the change in behavior. At that point, a "part" of the person was renamed. The renaming is the birth of the personality. Cults often attach demons to these personalities. That part of the person can have demons controlling it, without the host even knowing it.

Another way to invite evil possession is to **doubt or lack trust in God.** If a vacancy is created in the spiritual life, Satan is more than willing to fill the void. Often with promises of wealth or fame, demons move right in to take control. Threats are very common. Wrongs become right, rights become wrong. The father of lies believes he has conquered once again.

Dabbling in the occult, even if only "innocently" through occult influenced games, horoscopes, astrology or palm readings, opens the door for demons to come marching in.

The next major entrance of demon control is through a broad spectrum of sexual sin. Occult activity centers around sexual performances of the most degrading nature. Demons gain entry and control the person until he dies or is rescued by Christ. Generational transfers are made if the demon possessed person dies. The demon powers live on and must possess another body. Their most direct claims are the deceased person's children, grandchildren, or other close relatives, therefore being passed from generation to generation. The newly possessed will be tormented with lies that are intended to keep them captive. They are flooded with lies and assaults that they now belong to Satan and can never be free. Such lies are hard to overcome, as I have seen after working with numerous individuals who had been thus programmed. Christ can and does set them free with the proper guidance and time.

Alter-personalities can be successfully integrated as the host person matures emotionally and desires to be whole. Christian counselors who are trained and experienced in dealing with MPD can guide these patients through the process. With God's help, integration or release is possible. I have seen as hundreds of personalities become one person again. Integration or releasing means their job is over after they have given their memory or memories back to the host person to experience now as an adult. There is no longer a need for them to be separate or hidden or to conceal their secret.

As the memory is recalled, all of the physical and emotional pain is relived. The person may feel the same nausea, headache, smothering or pain that was present at the original abuse. It will be felt as if it were happening today. The stronger adult body can cope more easily than the child's body in previous years. The body can consciously deal with its own emotions. When this happens, the alter is integrated or released.

Integration is the goal of therapy. It simply means tuning each part to the same wave length or channel. An effective therapist can help clients reach such a goal; not overnight, but in time. The hard task for the therapists, counselors or friends is to help the victims to gain control of their lives again. Fear of recurring danger must be overcome.

Anger is often directed at themselves for not preventing what was happening. They blame themselves to the point of self-hatred, thinking of or attempting suicide or practicing self-mutilation: cutting themselves with knives or razor blades to see the blood flow, burning themselves or other self-torture.

In victims of SRA, this behavior may result from intense programming, and demons attached to cult-created personalities. Self-destructive behavior may take the form of anorexia, bulimia, or drug, alcohol or tobacco abuse. The anger may be directed toward others including parents, especially the mother, for not stopping the abuse. Some incidents that may at first appear to be self-destructive or self-mutilating behavior are indeed supernatural. Demons attached to cult-created personalities will cut, bruise, and claw the person. These claw marks can be anything from shallow scratches to deep, razor-sharp cuts, causing intense burning and bleeding. Even though a doctor's care and stitches might be advisable, most victims do not report these incidents or seek medical attention, knowing that most people will not believe the true source of their injuries.

After living an entire childhood in constant fear, the victims learn not to trust. They live in constant paralyzing fear because every time they trusted someone, they were hurt. As the abuse went on day after day, fear became their constant companion. They soon learned to fear and distrust everyone. They must realize which of their needs were not being met as a youngster, and make a place as an adult to meet their own needs without the assistance of the alters.

The good news is, healing is possible! These shattered pearls can become whole once more. Their color may vary like oyster pearls. For example, some black pearls are created inside the abalone. Pink pearls are sometimes found in conch shells. But they are each unique, wondrously beautiful, and certainly strong.

Rosealee told me recently, after her personalities had been integrated, "For the first time in my life, *I know that God loves me*. I had been told as a child that I was a bad and evil little girl. They said I could never go to heaven and that God did not love me, and I believed them. Now I know it was all a lie." She also said "Before, when I read the Bible, it never made sense. Now, when I read it, everything has a message for *me*."

Each victim of abuse appears breathtakingly beautiful when they emerge from the shell that held them captive. They are valued because of what they have become, despite their difficult life.

These pearls are special in that they have a unique story to tell. Each can help other persons who have similar backgrounds. These pearls of all different sizes and colors are treasures without a price tag!

(Note: The poems in this book were given to me by a shattered pearl who chose not to live. She took her life before I knew how to help her.)

I Want To Cry . . . Many Reasons!
by Heather

I WANT TO CRY - because he was my father.

I WANT TO CRY - because he stole my pride.

I WANT TO CRY - because I was born into slavery to my mother and father.

I WANT TO CRY - because he used with raw animalism.

I WANT TO CRY - because I had no options as a child.

I WANT TO CRY - because my home was not a refuge from the world.

I WANT TO CRY - because there was no smile on my pillow when I awoke.

I WANT TO CRY - because to be afraid was normal for me.

I WANT TO CRY - because he took advantage of my vulnerability.

I WANT TO CRY - 'because she confined me to an insecure world without any praise.

I WANT TO CRY - because he trapped me again and again.

I WANT TO CRY - for myself for all the years I wasn't willing nor able to stop rationalizing their behavior.

I WANT TO CRY - because I was robbed of the joy of Mother's Day and Father's Day.

I WANT TO CRY - for a long lost childhood.

I WANT TO CRY - because I believed them when they said I was bad.

I WANT TO CRY - because I was constantly rebuked and called a sinner and a loser.

I WANT TO CRY - for being forced to hide instead of playing when I was a little child.

I WANT TO CRY - for all the times I tried to kill myself because of their abuse.

Most of all, I WANT TO CRY - because they robbed me of the ABILITY TO CRY ...Is this reason enough to want to cry?

16

Implanted Or "False Memories"

(Plastic Pearls)

The Lord said to me, "The prophets are prophesying lies in my name. I have not sent them or appointed them or spoken to them. They are prophesying to you false visions, divinations, idolatries, and the delusions of their minds." Jeremiah 14:14

This is what the Lord Almighty says: "Do not listen to what the prophets are prophesying to you; they will fill you with false hopes. They speak visions from their own minds, not from the mouth of the Lord." Jeremiah 23:16

In recent years there has been much talk about a new and controversial subject. This twentieth century hot topic is called "False Memory Syndrome." The name in itself is a contradiction in terms. How can "memory" be "false?" What exactly is it then?

First, a little background: With the nineties also came a frenzied rush to therapist's offices. A society of "dysfunctionals" and "co-dependents" (also new terms) began seeking for answers or validation. Without knowing it, a new status symbol had been established. Much of the conversation at social events soon centered around who is seeing a therapist and how much better they feel about themselves. Soon it was acceptable and even expected for men, women and even children to have their own counselor or therapist. With the divorce rate soaring, divorcees and children began to question their self-worth and completeness and to blame themselves for lives gone wrong. Loss of jobs and the upsurge of health related problems also added to the population of clientele seeking third party counsel. Many have received much-needed and vital help when things were falling apart.

Unfortunately, not all therapists or counselors work by the same rules. With increased case loads, some have turned to quick diagnoses and solutions to the problems of their clientele. This has caused some to ignore the premise of good therapy technique.

The most effective counselor is a good listener for the client. On the other hand, the client must be open and honest about what is troubling them. In seeking to make a quick diagnosis, some therapists may suggest a scenario of abuse. The charge now is that some therapists are encouraging clients to manufacture histories of abuse. Is this possible? Yes, it can happen if several things are in place: First, if the client has read or watched movies, videos or television accounts of actual abuse or novels, and if suggestive therapy is used wherein leading or suggestive questions are asked.

Satan can and does plant thoughts in the minds of humans, if they have opened themselves up to his suggestions through doubts about the authority and power of God. Satan will use that doubt as an opportunity or invitation to project wrong thoughts into the mind.

The Bible tells us that Satan is the father of lies. "There is not truth in him. When he lies, he speaks his native language, for he is a liar and the father of lies." John 8:44.

One instance of planted falsehood is found in Nehemiah 6. The prophet was rebuilding the walls of Jerusalem. It seems the construction was almost complete, except for setting the gates. Sanaballat and Tobiah conspired to oppose the work. They sent a request for Nehemiah to meet them in one of the villages on the plain of Ono for a conference. Nehemiah sent word back that he was too busy with the work at hand to stop and go there. Four times, the message was sent with the same reply from the prophet. Finally, the fifth message came: "It is reported among the nations - and Geshem says it is true - that you and the Jews are plotting to revolt, and therefore, you are building a wall. Moreover, according to these reports, you are about to become their king and have even appointed prophets to make this proclamation about you in Jerusalem: `There is a king in Judah!' Now this report will get back to the king; so come let us confer together," Nehemiah 6:6-7.

In the next verse, Nehemiah replied, "Nothing like what you are saying is happening; you are just making it up out of your head," Nehemiah 6:8. However, the letters of intimidation intended to give him a bad name and discredit him continued. Their intent to cause the prophet to doubt God had failed. In verse 14, and onward, Nehemiah prayed for the plotters and the wall was competed "with the help of our God."

In spite of Satan's plot to thwart the progress, God's work was finished. The rumors had all been made up out of their own heads. The Evil One had successfully planted the falsehood. So convincing was it that all three of them believed it and repeated it for truth. Satan's agents are capable of making up and circulating falsehoods to discredit the work of God.

If there is someone to hurt or God's work to disrupt, Satan will plant falsehoods. These "false memories" are easy to detect if we use the advice given as a guide in the scriptures: "Try the Spirits," I John 4:1. If the policy of *test or try the spirit* is followed, what is true can readily be distinguished from all that is false. Emotions such as fear, terror and fright, as well as physical pain called body memories, are always a part of the recall process. The first time a memory is remembered, the body memories validate the original pain. During successive repeating of the incident, less and less body memories are manifested.

Repressed memories are not uncommon and should not be suspected of being made up memories. How many times have you asked someone a question about an incident that you know occurred and had the person say to you, "Oh, I forgot." No! Everything we have ever heard, read or seen is in our memory file, stored away in the gray matter. Proverbs 22:6 NIV says "Teach a child how he shall live and he will remember it all of his life." Studies have been done using laser to retrieve memories. One grown woman recalled in explicit detail the opera house in Vienna, Austria, where she had heard and seen an orchestral performance as a child of twelve. She described the rows of lights and even hummed several bars of the music.

Preserved in the sub-conscious memory are recordings from childhood, both events and feelings. Memory is aroused as keys or triggers are employed. The use of questions such as who, what, where, what do you feel, hear, see, smell, or taste, cause the victim of abuse to *reveal, not fabricate.* If a memory is repressed, this kind of questioning will be sufficient to open the locked files.

If there is no memory, nothing will come out! It has been stated that some therapists suggest topics and characters and ask the client to tell the story. If there is prior knowledge of abuse from reading or viewing, the creative ability can construct stories much like a novelist writing a book after doing his research. These incidents are usually told to the therapist in a matter of fact way, as if writing a news feature. Very little or no emotions are expressed.

On the other hand, when asked by a therapist, "What do *you* see, hear, feel, smell, etc.?", the client can go back into the memory file to the very place where the horrible incidents took place, reexperiencing all the physical and emotional pain and terror. Body memory is important when the conscious memory is filed away. For example, in some cases clients have shown unusual responses to hearing loud noises or certain odors. They were unaware that their responses were out of the ordinary. The body remembered when the conscious mind did not. Body memory can act as a reliable validation.

Trouble is caused to the psychotherapy field when "creations" are judged as real. Many innocent persons have been harmed, lives and careers ruined, and untold misery to family and friends has resulted. Lawsuits are now being waged against unscrupulous counselors, therapists and psychologists who are accused of asking suggestive or leading questions.

In the costume jewelry section of department stores, one can see fake "jewels" of all kinds. Here you will also find plastic pearls. Weight, color and size are what the shopper uses to judge their purchase. Color and size are easily duplicated or imitated. Weight, on the other hand, is not as easy. Plastic, because it is light weight, is very useful and versatile for the manufacture of many items. But the lack of weight is a sure giveaway when judging pearls. Another feature that could even make them dangerous is their susceptibility to fire and melting. True memories can stand the test and weight of validation where false memories cannot.

Many valid and true memories are judged as false by perpetrators who are feeling the heat of being found out. Well educated and respected community leaders have been guilty of abuse but personify an almost angelic presence to the public. In private or on the home front, the very opposite can be true. These abusers are insistent on proving these memories false and are suing therapists. The heat of lawsuits will cause false or implanted memories to melt and even catch fire.

A true memory cannot and will not melt or catch fire, even under pressure and testing. The vivid detail of some memories is beyond question. Accuracy of revealed information known only to the abused and the abuser cannot be made up.

Some have been eager to disprove all repressed memories as false. While the memories of my own childhood abuse were never forgotten, I see many who do have repressed memories. When they find a safe place to open the file cabinet of their mind, these memories pour out in detailed accuracy. Some examples are descriptions of furnishings, temperature, odors, tastes and even wallpaper patterns. The mind will not be able to bring out what it does not have filed away. As some cry "False Memory," their victims may retract or drop charges of real abuse rather than deal with the injustice in the system or the embarrassment of going through the process time.

Some have suggested that these are delusions caused by demons. As we look into the scriptures, we are asked "Can a house divided against itself stand?" See Luke 11:14-23. All evil, including the abuse of children, begins with the influence of Satan. Many innocent children have been victimized *by humans who were under the influence of Satan*. This does not make the victim demonic! Children have been used by adults without their willing participation. Willful misconduct is *sin*. Forced submission is *victimization*. A fact closer to the truth is that the demon in the abuser will protest "false memory" in order to keep the real truth from surfacing, and will make the accuser appear mentally deficient.

Why is it so hard for people to believe an adult could have repressed memories? Post Traumatic Stress Disorder (PTSD) can be caused by rape, torture, sexual abuse, severe physical injury, natural disasters, earthquakes, flood, fire, the tragic death of a loved one, or military combat.

For example, if you have ever followed a veteran of combat, you will note that it was also possible for these grown men to bury deeply their emotional wounds of war. Young soldiers were not prepared to see their buddies dropping all around them, mowed down by enemy machine gun fire. One such soldier, 28 years after a battle in Vietnam, explained it this way: "I was wounded in the jaw, leg and back. Dead men were all around me and one fell on top of me. I barely hung onto reality to keep from going insane." He had to focus on staying alive and sane. Not until years later did he face the reality of what had happened. Then it was safe to feel the pain and to weep, really weep.

In training, he was warned about the possibilities of casualties, but when he saw his closest friend with his head blown open, the reality was worse than he could ever have imagined. In order to make it through the skirmishes and off the battlefield, the soldier had to block all visual images from consciousness. His own safety depended upon his "keeping his cool." To break down emotionally was not permitted. It was better to place the memory in a file and live solely for today.

Years later, the emotional impact of those tragic scenes may return with full force. Like splashes of cold water in the face, the memories recur; in flashbacks at first, then the whole picture emerges. The soldier once again feels like he is on the battlefield with all the sights, sounds and smells, but now his emotions need not be harnessed. Tears flood the eyes and big men cry unashamed tears for friends long departed. Yet no one dares accuse these soldiers of manufacturing a false memory.

PTSD can cause isolation, fears, withdrawal, lack of interest in normal living and activities, anger, memories and flashbacks, impulsive behaviors, nightmares or recurrent bad dreams. Physical symptoms can include panic attacks, sweating, heart palpitations, chills, and many unexplained symptoms. A survivor may have the feeling of being abandoned or betrayed by others. This often leads to depression.

Dissociative Disorders can also be caused by a terrible car accident. If the pain is so bad that the person cannot bear it, the accident victim may dissociate or split. By giving the pain to another personality or personalities, they are then able to go through treatment, surgery, and recovery of an otherwise unbearable incident. PTSD may not be evident until many years later. I've known persons who still have not recalled violent accidents in which they were injured critically.

These same types of memories are recalled by victims of child abuse. Their battlefields were also very real. Even though there were no newsmen or third party records to validate the place and time, the skirmishes took place and destruction occurred. Adult abusers waged vicious war on innocent children. As these children became adults themselves, the abusers envision taking them on as peers and attempt to discredit the victim's memories. They cry "False Memory Syndrome" and expect all the world to listen.

It is time to believe the victim, whether child or adult. Here is one simple question that should be asked: What does the victim have to gain by claiming these memories anyway? It is embarrassing to admit what happened. It has kept many victims silent for decades. It has no rewards. And it is certainly not anything like winning the lottery to go public! So, I ask again: What does the victim have to gain by claiming an untrue memory? That is it: Nothing! Especially is this true when the victim's parents or other abusers are dead. There is no one to sue, no gain, only the emptying of the pain inside.

Dedicated christian counselors can have assurance in distinguishing true from false if they make God their partner at all times. God will give the gifts of knowledge, insight, and discernment to those who truly seek to be used for God's glory alone. *(See I Corinthians 12:1, 7-10)*

"And afterward I will pour out my Spirit on all people. Your sons and daughters will prophesy, your old men will dream dreams, your young men will see visions. Even on my servants, both men and women, I will pour out my Spirit in those days", Joel 2:28-29.

"The Sovereign Lord has given me an instructed tongue, to know the word that sustains the weary. He wakens me morning by morning, wakens my ear to listen like one being taught. The Sovereign Lord has opened my ears, and I have not been rebellious, I have not drawn back", Isaiah 50:4-5.

The real question is "false memory or repressed memory?" Repressed memories are only locked away, waiting for a safe place and time to be revealed. Real memories, though once repressed, are not plastic pearls!

It's Raining In My Heart
by Heather

They tell me that I'm older now -
To laugh! to smile! have lots to say!
My days of schools and books are past!
So throw my cares away!
Well, maybe the sun is shining,
And no clouds are in the sky!
Maybe each flower is visited
By a lovely butterfly -
Maybe birds are singing and
The fruit is on the vine . . .
But how can I love flowers
And radiant sunshine . . .
When it's raining in my heart?
All I see is rain clouds
And shadows hanging low.
The sunshine is my enemy,
The flowers are my foe.
I envy everyone's happiness,
I wish it were my own -
But until I find that happiness,
Why can't they leave me alone?
Someday soon, perhaps I'll laugh
And love the summer once again,
I'll make up for time lost now,
But until then . . .
It's raining in my heart . . .

17

Disclosure Procedures

Finding Pearls

Ten to fifteen years ago, 250,000 new cases of incest were reported each year with victims ranging in age from a few months to 18 years. Many more cases are currently being reported each year. Unfortunately, most disclosure or reporting of the abuse is done only after the victim has become an adult. Many years may have passed and more victims can be tallied against the same offender. The statute of limitations varies from state to state and unless the offender is still violating children, it may be impossible to take legal action against him or her for earlier offenses.

Quite often, victims begin to deal with their past only after they have become adults. Feeling that the threats that kept them silent as children are no longer valid, they may begin to confront their past. Therapy and counseling are costly and it is unreasonable for the victim to bear this cost alone. Suing for damages may be the only way to retrieve some of the expenditures.

Since the victim has been quiet for many years, the abuser believes his offenses will not be revealed. But we have read "Be sure your sin will find you out," or in another version, "You can be sure your sin will find you out," Numbers 32:23. Just when the abuser thinks he has gotten away with it, or that it is no longer a threat or maybe forgotten, BOOM! The story is exposed.

Former Miss America, Marilyn Adler, speaking at a seminar, said "You *will* be found out. Your victim will speak your name. You may be alive or dead but your secret will be exposed." How true! Luke 12:1-3 NIV says ". . . They were trampling on one another, Jesus began first to speak to his disciples (the church) saying . . . there is nothing concealed that will not be disclosed, or hidden that will not be made known. What you have said in the dark will be heard in the daylight, and what you have whispered in the ear in the inner rooms will be proclaimed from the roofs."

The secrets are being proclaimed from the roofs, by means of television antennas, on the evening news and on talk shows. They are being printed in the newspapers. Offenders do not comprehend the seriousness of the charges and are often surprised when they are brought to light.

Assault leaves victims with residual feelings about their completeness or wholeness. Scarring is deep and long lasting. As a child of thirteen, I had no knowledge of where babies came from. Until then, I had not wanted to know. When my father began deep kissing and fondling me, I was sure this must be how you got pregnant. Knowing the embarrassment it would cause me and my family, I fled in tears to my room and cried myself to sleep. Now the secret is being proclaimed from the printed page as well as through the airways. This will give others permission to tell. Telling the secret will make offenders accountable for their actions.

What happens when incest comes to light? Mothers are alienated from daughters, sisters are afraid to talk, siblings withdraw from each other, friends withdraw from friends, and sons hate their fathers. The secrecy code that the family has abided by causes separation, alienation and isolation from other family and friends at a time when they could bring the greatest amount of strength to one another. (from "Integrated treatment of Child Abuse")

To prevent alienation, education is essential. If you suspect abuse, the following steps are suggested for dealing with children who may have been sexually abused:

1. If your child tells you someone is trying to or has molested them, believe and support them. Commend the child for telling you and carefully explain that you understand and support them.

2.   Avoid emotional interrogations and statements such as, "I just can't believe this is happening." Do not ask the child, "Why didn't you tell me sooner?" This only lays more guilt on the child. Encourage instead, by saying "I know how scary it must have been to tell me this."

3.   If the child tells you something that indicates sexual abuse, calmly ask questions. Assure them you will help, but do not put words in the child's mouth. Put them at ease by telling them there is no need to be embarrassed. Assure them that they did noting wrong, nor did they cause the abuse in any way.

4.   Do not express any extreme reactions such as anger or shock when you hear of a molestation attempt. Do not threaten physical harm to the perpetrator. The child needs a calm protector who doesn't unduly frighten with anger or hysteria.

5.   Do not accuse the child of trying to break up the family. Do not threaten scary consequences such as "Dad will go to jail" or "We won't have any money to buy food." Calmly accept what the child is saying, and do not react in front of the child.

6.   Support the child by what you do and say. Tell the child that he or she is not to blame for what happened.

7.   Do not smother the child with your affection or by repeatedly saying how terrible the abuse has been. The child could come to believe that there is no recovery from molestation.

8.   Be sure the child knows that he or she will be protected from further attempts of abuse. Provide the child with a physically and emotionally safe environment in which to recover.

9.   Do not blame or condemn yourself for what has happened. The abuser is the only guilty party.

10. Report the suspected molestation to a social service agency or the police. It is critical that you take action, no matter who the molester may be. If nothing is done, the child and other children will continue to be at risk of further harm.

11. DO NOT REMOVE THE CHILD! The Court, or Department of Human Services should not be allowed to remove the abused child from his home. That kind of action only traumatizes the child again. It punishes the child for the sins of the

fathers. The child is the one who is made to suffer separation from his family. This reinforces what the abuser has told them: "If you tell, you will be taken away," or "Everyone will know YOU have been a bad boy or girl if you tell anyone about it."

Children should be allowed to stay in familiar surroundings. Their young lives should not be disrupted again. THE ABUSER, whether father or mother, SHOULD BE REMOVED, and not allowed to be alone with the child again. More damage and trauma is brought about by needless removal of the child. Confusion and disruption of the child's routine are the results of such actions. The child is again the loser! He or she loses everything familiar: surroundings, including their own room and bed, associations of friends, and the comfort of those who care about them, including non-abusive parents, siblings and grandparents.

Children are not property, to be moved about at will like pawns, as if they have no feelings nor need for security and emotional health. There is no need to move them around like furniture. When adults abuse, why should children be the ones to pack and leave? When there is a non-offending parent in the home, the child should be allowed to remain in familiar surroundings, as far as possible. Only in a situation where BOTH parents are abusers should arrangements be made for the child to leave the home they know.

12. Find a specialized agency, therapist, or doctor with appropriate expertise to evaluate the sexual abuse. When a child is molested, family members are under great stress. They may need to discuss their situation with an objective professional specifically trained and practiced in dealing with children and their families.

If sexual abuse is properly dealt with while children are young, they will not have to face a life of pain and shame like those who do not confront their abuse until years later.

YOUNG PEARLS - HANDLE WITH CARE!

111

18

The Pearl Process

Pearls Aplenty

This process of creating pearls represents a somewhat forced partnership between man and mollusk. Relying on the ability of the small shellfish to secrete micro-layers of protective coating around the foreign object, a pearl is almost guaranteed. Culturing makes them more available and thus, more affordable. For long centuries, the pearl has been a symbol of virtue, wisdom, and wealth. For romantics, the pearl has symbolized purity, chastity and feminine charm.

In the cultured pearl farming process, if 100 oysters are seeded, an average of fifty percent may die or reject the "seed". About twenty will produce marketable pearls. Less than five will produce true gems.

All abuse victims are affected differently as well. For many, the incident may be passed off as a growing experience, especially if the offender was a sibling. These persons were neither threatened with harm nor told to keep silent. Thus, they were spared the long-lasting shame of dealing with the incident as a sexual experience.

On the other hand, for the majority of abuse victims, it was an incident of violent or forced abuse, causing greater and longer lasting harm. The feeling of helplessness and betrayal can pervade and color their entire view of life. Every relationship they encounter is tainted with distrust and shame as a result of their past abuse.

Timing The Pearl

Before 1960, oysters were kept in the water for two and one-half years after being seeded. At that time, one year was dropped from the culturing time. Since 1979, culturing has taken only six to eight months.

By using a larger "seed" or nuclei, a pearl of a decent size is acquired. However, the lasting value of such pearls has been greatly reduced as well. Since they are the softest of gem stones, thinly coated pearls won't last long enough to pass down to another generation. Nacre thickness being so shallow, they will crack, discolor, and become worthless.

Victims of sexual abuse need time to process the violation done to them physically and emotionally. Persons who have not suffered in such a way believe recovery should take less time that it does. For each individual, the time varies. Processing time depends on a wide range of circumstances. Age when the abuse occurred, frequency and duration of abuse, level of violence involved in the incident, offender's relationship to the victim, emotional threats surrounding the incidents and support system once the disclosure occurs, all influence the time needed for recovery.

Therapy cannot be rushed, nor a time set for completion. With each individual, the abuse is different. Therefore, recovery cannot be predetermined. For some, very little time is needed, while others may take years. Methods also vary. Reading and journaling may be all that is necessary for some persons. Other individuals may need one to three or more years with a therapist to deal with the reality that life can have meaning again. Prayer and Bible reading may be all some require. Support groups are valuable to some while still others may require a combination of methods. Whatever method is needed, the timing cannot be rushed. The value and durability of these pearls depend on each individual choosing the method and timing that is right for them.

One of the greatest forms of therapy is speaking out against abuse. By doing so, you in turn give permission or freedom to others to step out of their self-blame and self-shame. More and more recovered persons are needed to meet the needs of those still suffering in silence. Educational degrees are helpful, but not always necessary. A good listener who has been through the same pain is the most valuable of all therapists. Never underestimate what you can do to help suffering humanity! Remember,

"Little is much, if dedicated to God." His children, young and old, are depending upon your experience.

As the pearl's size is determined by the diameter of the nucleus, the kind and length of abuse can influence the strength of our "pearl." Natural pearls might have grown ten to twenty years, thus creating larger and stronger gems. Now, because of so much pollution in the water, the life of the oyster may be in danger if kept in the water too long.

Long, drawn out therapy may be of little value. Some group therapy or "meeting" type groups may cause an addiction to "support." Year after year of constant involvement in such programs could pollute the water, thus stifling real growth. Group programs are necessary for some to realize they are not alone in their suffering, but are not a valid solution by themselves.

The Sea of Galilee is a small but active body of water. It is fed by a constant stream of fresh water from the melting snows of Mount Hermon. In it are fish of many kinds. It supports many fishermen in the area. Hundreds of thousands of tourists enjoy the seafood in the restaurants that surround the small body of water. Water is constantly coming into the sea and the Jordan River flows out of the south end to feed the thirsty, fertile farmland and the towns of 4.7 million people living along its banks.

65 miles due south as the crow flies, or 160 twisting miles of river bed later, the Jordan River is reduced to a small stream which empties into the Dead Sea. As the name indicates, it is dead. The Dead Sea cannot support any living thing. It keeps what it has and receives. It gives no nourishment to animals, plants or mankind. It has no outlet and therefore does not continue to flow. The hot desert sun evaporates the water instead, leaving behind a sea of brackish, bitter, salty water. As pretty and clear as it may appear, it quenches no thirsty traveler. The only thing it does provide is a playground where curious tourists come to soak up sun. Of course, they take pictures of each other "swimming" in water you cannot sink in because of the high concentration of mineral salts.

Long term support group therapy should only be a means to an end and not an end in itself. Constantly receiving while not giving can encourage participants to become stagnant and even bitter. Year after year of attending meetings is much like treading water. It is true that you can't sink as long as you are in the group, but there is a need for recovered individuals to share their recovery with others. If it is not our shame, why is it still being hidden? Confidentiality is necessary only in the early stages of recovery. After that, we only continue to protect the offender's secret by our silence. By giving, we can remain sweet and strong. The Jordan River, giving all along its journey, continues to support life until it empties itself into the Dead Sea.

I do not wish to condemn the value of "twelve-step" programs or support groups in any way. I conduct them myself, especially for the early stages of recovery. These should be places for being fed and launched into serving others who are in pain. Their value cannot be measured. But more valuable is the service to the world they can provide once participants emerge from behind the closed doors. Participants should talk about their own recovery only. Privacy of others should be carefully guarded. The goal should be that, in time, each one can reach that same level of emotional growth, ready to share with and encourage others.

We are not what we were, but neither are we all we can become. We can show the world that we are rich and valuable pearls by letting them see what we have become despite where we have been.

Pearls Of Many Colors

Abuse victims become "pearls of many colors." Child abuse does not happen to just one race or nationality, or in only one country or location. Speaking at an international convention several years ago confirmed this for me. Participants from all around the world came to me following the lecture. The same problems have surfaced all over the globe.

It is logical then that we would find a large variety of pearl colors. In America, many have begun to speak out about abuse. Now, from around the world, others are following our example. Customs vary in other countries and sexual abuse is not recognized for what it is, neither is it illegal.

This is true in some providences of third world countries. One such example is in Africa where some men marry many wives. If the wife is pregnant, the husband is not to have sex with her. So he has many wives, or has sex with his daughter, sisters or cousins. In that culture, it is not considered incest. However, we in America cry out otherwise. Those young girls hurt just the same as children in this country. A missionary wife on furlough brought this to my attention recently. She took some of my seminar material back to her mission. Writing within a few weeks, she said "I never dreamed I would have to use your material so soon." Children from all around the world are exposed to adult information far too soon. Pearls of many colors are emerging from the brackish waters of societies around the globe.

One french pearl dealer boasted of 22,000 black pearls in his annual harvest. Of the millions of cases of abuse reported annually in this country, there is no breakdown by race, but there are more colors of pearls than ever before. If one speaks out, others will follow, of all colors.

Rape, Hardcore Pain - Tarnished Pearls

In addition to sand or an inserted bead as a nucleus for a pearl, it is possible for a small snail or a parasite to bore through the shell. The end product then is pearlized just the same as a round bead. It could be shaped like a snail shell but have the appearance of pearl, unique but beautiful.

The parasite or intruder reminds me of the work of rapists who bore into innocent lives with violence, anger and force. The victim is violated and left emotionally dead. He or she can let the experience destroy them or they can become a stronger person. There is no reason to allow what happened in our past to control our tomorrows. The pearl developed because of a parasite is no less beautiful or valuable.

Victims of rape must process not only the power issue, but often the violence associated with rape. They experience the same violation and self-blame. If they are not murdered in the attack, they too may be threatened or forced into silence for fear the attacker may return to finish the job.

Rape is an act of violence, not sex. Rape victims must not blame themselves for the attack. While many rape victims are adults, it is still never their fault that the rape occurred. Regardless of threats, if the victim would report the incident, and make positive identification, an arrest could be made and the rapist could be punished and also receive the help he needs. Recovery would occur much sooner for the victim once it was reported and the offender was no longer a threat. That does not mean that he or she will not have nightmares and other symptoms throughout the process but reporting facilitates reality therapy.

This pearl may be a little different shape than pearls from childhood abuse but it is no less a beautiful gem. This gem has a valuable place in our world, helping others through similar experiences. Our own recovery takes place sooner if we can help someone else in their recovery. We can be seen as a person of power, in control again. Rape need not rob us of a satisfying future. Don't be ashamed to let the world see you as a unique pearl in control of a once-shattered life. Remember, tarnished pearls can be polished, renewed and returned to their original beauty.

Nature's Work Of Art - Costly Pearls

The pearl industry has large numbers of employees, from divers to graders, and equipment is needed to operate the business. Thus, the pearl farmer has made large investment in his business. Financial investment, size, time and color all influence the cost of a pearl. The oyster I purchased in the see-through can cost approximately ten dollars-not a large outlay of cash for the pearl I found inside. However, the farmer who boasted of 22,000 black pearls got much more than ten dollars each for them.

China leads the world in the production of freshwater pearls, producing 50 to 80 tons each year. A necklace may contain approximately 56 pearls at a cost of $1,000.00, or $18.00 per pearl. Larger single pearls may bring up to $1,000.00 each, depending on size.

Black or white South Sea pearls can sell for $4,000.00 to $40,000.00 each. A strand of 30 of these gems is very expensive indeed. A single 13 millimeter round pearl easily sells for $10,000.00. Japan's marine product export is worth more than $300,000,000.00 annually.

The value of abuse pearls cannot be calculated. No bank could hold the worth of one of these pearls. Someone has said, "a lost childhood is vanished forever," How true! No amount of money and therapy can recapture innocence.

Not all uses of the pearl in the past were esoteric. Aborigines of Australia, who accidently cracked their teeth while feeding on oysters, considered pearls an inconvenience. Their children used the "worthless" nuisances for marbles. American Hopewell indians collected them by the thousands to adorn themselves or accompany their dead in crematories and funeral mounds.

Kokichi Mikimoto, who died in 1954 at the age of 96, boasted that he owed his health to the two pearls he swallowed every morning. The pharmaceutical branch of his company grinds pearls and shells into calcium carbonate tablets. Tons of tiny or flawed pearls are ground up to go into medicines, cosmetics and tooth paste each year, but even one victim of child abuse is too valuable a pearl to be discarded or ignored!

Finishing The Pearl - Natural Beauty

Pearls need no polishing or cutting to reveal their beauty. They were once the most valued of all gems, until the early 19th century when diamonds gained in popularity. The pearl, as it comes from the shell, is complete in its beauty. Cleaned only with fresh salt and water, it is ready to be sized and marketed.

Therapy does not polish, cut or shape, but only discovers pearls. Counselors or therapists provide comfortable environments and tools to reveal these pearls.

The color of the pearl that emerges from the shell may be cream, pink, silver, blue, green, yellow, or black. What causes this difference in color is a mystery that has been studied for over 80 years. Oysters are capable of producing more than one pearl. Pearl farmers are still baffled by the fact that an oyster with five shell nuclei and five pieces of mantle from the same sacrificed oyster could produce five different colored pearls.

Individuals from the same school or community may have been abused as children, unbeknown to each other. Only as adults, when they speak out, do they find the common thread of their existence. Even though raised in the same environment, children of many races emerge as pearls of many colors. The true miracle in the whole pearl process is the outstanding beauty that emerges from such an unalluring origin!

Dear Professional

by Heather . . . The Patient

We do the things you want,
    and take your healing pill,
We ask you great professional
    "Do you know how we feel?"

With Freudian techniques,
    and Gestalt as well,
You can walk through the chambers
    that lead to "our" hell.

Through Positive thinking
    and staying alert -
You seem to be saying -
    "We can end all that hurt."

Walk a mile down the corridor
    that leads through our minds,
But be prepared for the horrors
    we know you will find

Go first from a baby
    with booties so sweet;
To a twelve year old child
    with big clumsy feet . . .

Watch as the cooing
    turns into screams,
And watch as the nightmares
    replace the sweet dreams!

Watch as the little child
    with sad hurting eyes . . .
Stifles the terrors,
    and smothers the cries.

Watch as her father,
    with evil control
Rapes her small body,
    while raping her soul!

Watch as the same child,
        her heart full of rage
Learns to distrust,
        no matter what age.

What can she do,
        with fears of her own,
Except build a world
        to live in "alone?"

You say "bonding"
        is the magical word.
In her childlike mind,
        that's really absurd!

Abuse was a comrade
        a most vicious foe!
You claim to have answers,
        but how would you know?

You've learned from your textbooks,
        and listened quite well!
You know the mechanics,
        Oh, that we can tell!

We want freedom of will,
        we want freedom of choice.
If we must take your pill,
        or listen to your voice.

Don't be condescending,
        don't look down your nose!
Because in reality my friend,
        this is how it goes!

WE ARE YOUR TEACHERS,
        just give us a chance.
When the small coos vanish,
        will you save us a dance?

19

No More Denial, Please

(Victorious Pearls)

The afternoon of Jesus' healing of the sick and teaching his followers was interrupted by shouts of scorn. "Here is this woman we caught in adultery" they stormed. Jesus no doubt wondered, just as we have, "Where is the man?" Adultery is not a solo activity! They troubled themselves greatly to bring the woman to Jesus for reproof, but conveniently let the man slip out the back door; back to his office, back to his home, back to the temple . . . back where?

Mary, the woman, scarcely given enough time to dress, faced an accusing audience. Her eyes met the eyes of the master, eyes filled with pity and compassion. Her heart, full of shame, bowed low before a Holy God.

Jesus, a Master of crowd control, spoke not a word, but silently stooped to the ground. The restless mob, anxious to see how he was going to handle this scandal, pressed in for a closer look. In the sand, Jesus began to write. "What is he doing?" they asked. "What is he writing?" they whispered hoarsely. As they stepped forward, many faces reddened with shame. Right there before them, written in the sand for all the crowd to see, were their own sins. Perhaps some of this very mob were guilty of visiting Mary as darkness fell over the street. They had assumed their secrets were safe. No one would know. No one would tell. No one had seen, or so they thought. Now, written before them by an all-knowing God, was their name and their sins. One by one, the crowd fell away. Simon, who had first led the young girl into sin, blushed and slipped out of the circle of onlookers.

Years before, Mary, then only a child herself, had looked upon Simon as a trusted friend. He was respected by her family and she never suspected he would betray her trust. Knowing the power of the relationship, he took advantage of her innocence. As is the case of many sexually abused young girls, promiscuity followed. Her only power was in being in control of the situation. She had something the men of the city wanted. In prostitution, she could say when and for how much.

Ninety percent of prostitutes were victims of sexual abuse or incest in the home. Mary was no exception. Her young heart, broken by shame, felt no respect for herself. What followed was a life of secret affairs. As the word was passed along, Mary soon became the talk of the town. Men streamed to her door.

It must have been some "self-respecting" businessmen, deciding to expose the ring of prostitution, that burst into Mary's suite. They had watched her door from the shadows and they knew she would not be alone. "Ah-ha! So this is how you trap the men of the city and bring ruin to our neighborhood! Come with us. Wrap your robe about you and be hasty. You should be ashamed of yourself. We are going to see what Jesus has to say about this!"

Only Jesus didn't say anything; not one word! With his finger, he wrote in the sand the names and sins of her accusers, and one by one, they left. Standing there alone before Jesus, her sin was so ugly that she wanted to hide. As she stood there shaking, a soft, kind voice gently asked, "Where are your accusers?"

"There are none, Lord. They all left."

"Well Mary, neither do I condemn you. Go my child and don't do it again."

With grateful heart, she left. Her feet danced with joy as she returned to her apartment. Never again would she entertain men in her bed. Jesus had given her back the self-respect stolen by Simon. Now she could open the curtains and allow the sun to cast out the shadows of her home too. No longer was it necessary to hide behind darkened windows. No longer would she have to hang her head in the market place.

Mary found new employment and a new life for herself. Ever grateful to her Savior, she thought nothing of the cost of the gift she bought for him. She poured the exquisite perfume on his feet and wiped them with her hair. Her tears of joy and gratefulness were mingled with the fragrance that filled the room. Forever was she thankful to a God who could release her from a life of abuse and wrong choices.

When her accusers had walked away from the writing in the sand, they denied their own sin. By walking away, they were hiding their heads in the sand. They refused to admit and face their guilt. In fact, they denied the reality of their sin. Denial is also the response to any suggestion that such things happen in the church today.

Christians tend to believe that when they are baptized, they are immune to sin, that the baptismal font inoculates and insulates them against Satan's temptation. Actually, the contrary is true. As soon as a child of God is baptized, his warfare against evil begins. Satan works the hardest with Christians, ever tempting and snaring them to do evil. What happens behind closed doors is hidden from fellow church people. Children are kept silent about what takes place by threats of harm, so to fellow Christians, it cannot be true.

These Christians especially remind me of the three monkeys called See No Evil, Hear No Evil, Speak No Evil. If they do not see it or hear it or speak it themselves, then it just doesn't exist. So-called Christian offenders are masters of denial. Their stories are so believable that they deceive whole congregations. The congregations, in turn, believe the pious appearance of the offender over the word of innocent children. Even years later, when these children, now grown to adulthood, expose the evil done to them, they are scorned and not believed. Denial by the offender is the expected response. Denial by fellow church people is a learned response, taught by the deceiver himself. As Christians, it is time to realize there are Judases and Simons in our congregations!

In I Corinthians 5:1, the Apostle Paul wrote to the Christians in Corinth, "It is actually reported that there is sexual immorality among you and of a kind that does not happen even among the pagans . . . " This was a message to the church. No one else, not even the pagans, read or heard this reproof. It was addressed to the Christians. Paul recognized that sin was taking place in the church and did not choose to overlook it as some fellow Christians and church leaders do.

In verse 2, he continued "And you are proud! Shouldn't you rather have been filled with grief and have put out of your fellowship the man who did this?" In verse 5 he added, "Hand him over to Satan so that his sinful nature can be destroyed and his spirit be saved." In other words, hold this man accountable so that he can be saved.

Don't deny this is happening by turning the monkey's deaf ear and blind- eye. Hold him accountable if you really care about him, if you care about his eternal salvation. In verse 12, Paul went on to say he was not writing this to those outside of the church. "What business is it of mine to judge those outside the church? Are you not to judge those inside?"

Believe the children! It can easily be judged whether a child is telling the truth by asking a few questions. Children do not make up details without prior knowledge and experience unless they are coached by an adult or they have read or seen it somewhere. Read and re-read the chapter of this book on prevention, to protect the children in the church and home. "Speak up for the people who cannot speak for themselves. Protect the rights of all who are helpless," Proverbs 31:8, NIV. You, the church, are to speak up for and protect the children.

Physical, emotional and sexual abuse does happen in Christian homes and churches, at the hands of apparently consecrated parents and leaders. Condemnation alone is not the answer. Condemnation tends to foster further denial. Believe and rescue the children. Rescue the abuser by holding him accountable if you care about his soul. Look for the pearl hidden in the abuser's heart, as well. "Two are better than one because they have a good return for their work: If one falls down, his friend can help him up. but pity the man who falls and has no one to help him up," Ecclesiastes 4:9-10, NIV.

Only as we recognize we are in a warfare against evil, even within the church, can we gather the forces to battle. It is a hand-to-hand conflict with Satan himself. We must call upon the hand of God and all the holy angels to help us overcome the evil one. "With God on our side, who can stand against us?"

The victory is the Lord's! Victorious pearls will at last be gathered home. "They will be mine," says the Lord Almighty, "in the day when I make up my treasured possession," Malachi 3:17.

Lord, Heal The Child

by Heather

If I were you and you were me,
Would you see the world the way I see?
Or would you look in deep disgrace
As the tears roll down my face?
Would you gaze in deep despair
And think the wold was so unfair?
Judge me small, so you'll be tall.
Judge me not and avoid hurts fall.
You can't judge me and still be fair.
You weren't there to fill my chair.
I asked for love, they gave me hate.
I asked for peace, Oh! my mistake.
A tiny face looked up with fear.
They never wiped away my tears!
Never a kiss, never a hug!
Only a tug on the proverbial rug.
I tried to love her. I tried to be kind.
I offered my heart, she tortured my mind!
INCEST to my father, was his natural way.
I sit here all broken and stressful today.
One hug would have healed me,
Had it come from the heart.
But, his hugs were all dirty,
And they tore me apart.
I close my eyes tightly,
And say a little prayer.
Lord, heal the child inside
That I know is hiding there.
Bring back hope to this frail heart
And help me make a brand new start . . .
Lord, Jesus, if you see
The broken heart inside of me,
Let love flow from your throne,
So I won't feel so all alone.
Take the hurt and take the pain.
Give me sunshine in place of rain.
And I will serve you everyday.
In Jesus lovely name I pray. Amen.

127

20

Gates Of Pearl

Chapters 21 and 22 of Revelation give us a description of the Holy City. When the redeemed at last reach their reward as overcomers, we will be welcomed into our new home, the Holy City. The foundations of the city are constructed of precious jewels of jasper, sapphire, chalcedony, emerald, sardonyx, carnelian, chrysolite, beryl, topaz, chrysophase, jacinth and amethyst. The walls are of transparent gold. But the most amazing construction material described is that of the gates to the New Jerusalem. In Revelation 21:21, we learn that the way into the city is through the gates of PEARL! According to John, each gate is a single pearl. All the pearls I have seen are no bigger than a June pea.

What is the message we are to derive from this description? Certainly no oyster, nor even a giant clam, could produce a pearl large enough to fashion a gate of that magnitude. The size of the gate is no garden-gate either. There are twelve gates, all identical in size. These gates must be large enough to accommodate the large crowd; not an unruly crowd like we might expect to see going into a sporting event or a musical performance, but one with no pushing and shoving and no one being trampled under foot. The gates will be opened wide to receive all of the redeemed who number as the sands of the sea. The walls of the city, by the description given, are about 1,500 miles along each of the four sides. Twelve gates surround the city, thus making them approximately 500 miles apart. This is not talking of a gate or door only a few inches thick either. With walls approximately 200 feet thick, we can only imagine the size of these gates of pearl!

Now, envision the enormous pearl used to fashion such a huge gate. God's hand is not short where His children are concerned. He has planned a reward that no earthly father could ever dream of. See Malachi 3:17.

As the light of God and the Son shines upon the gates, we will see with our own eyes the iridescent colors emanating from each. But why a pearl? Could it be that our Father, knowing the pain and suffering His children will pass through, planned this ultimate reward?

There are some who have suffered persecution for their faith and died as martyrs. A great number have experienced the pain of physical illness. There will be faithful men and women who lived their Christian lives before an unbelieving spouse and prayed without ceasing. An untold number of men, women and children will have given up their lives in wars. In her book "Early Writings," page 19, E. G. White mentions "an innumerable company of little ones." Could these be children who were aborted or died at the hands of evil men in satanic rituals or in violent homes?

Victims of sexual abuse will especially appreciate the beauty of gates of pearl. Overcoming great pain and difficulty while on earth, we will at last find a safe haven beyond the Pearly Gates in a place where there will be no night, no fear, no shame, no pain, and no evil.

A loving Savior will be there also to welcome us home. He and our guardian angel will at last reveal the number of tears they too shed because we were being hurt.

The Holy Spirit will make known to us the strength He gave us to overcome the pain and shame. A **REAL** Father, the God of love and protection, will reach out His arms of acceptance to His once bruised children who have become real Pearls. The search is over! The victims become "VICTORS" as they walk through the gates of Pearl.

Appendix

After Words...

I dreamed I was somehow in a crowd, mostly of women. We had each been given a dusty blue dress which reminded me of a hospital gown. They were very plain, sewn down on both sides and just dropped over our heads. Also, we had soft rubber sandals similar to flip-flops, which had laces instead of straps.

We were put through some kind of paces like calisthenics; twisting, turning and some on the floor where we had to roll up. We pinched our dresses closed between our legs as we went through the exercises on the floor.

I noticed that my sandals fit me. Mine were just about the size of my feet while the others had shoes almost twice their size. They stumbled and walked very awkwardly. I thought if I laced mine up tighter and neater, I might get around even better. I reasoned the others could too, but I didn't say anything. If they saw me, they would get the hint and lace theirs up tighter for a better fit.

While I was lacing up my sandals, I heard a group behind me (I didn't know who they were) saying rather sarcastically, "I wonder if she can lace up the sergeant's jacket that well." With that, I was thrown a very large jacket with laces on it. I started at the bottom and laced it up neatly. When I was finished, it was taken from me and given back to the sergeant, who was going to put it on, or so I thought.

But when I looked up, the sergeant was putting on a brilliant white shirt with rows and rows of small pleats about five inches across and rows and rows of pearl buttons. The buttons were to hold the pleats in place. It looked like an impossible job so I stepped up and began helping him fasten the buttons. I had only buttoned a few of the rows when he spoke. Matter-of-factly, but with much emphasis, he questioned "<u>When</u> are you going to . . ." I thought I was about to be scolded. Then he continued, "When are you going to marry me and let me take you out of the maddening place?" With my hands still busy fastening buttons, I leaned back at arms length, looked up at him, and in the same tone, I asked, "When are you going to ask me?" His hands gripped my shoulders as he asked, "Will you marry me?" It was like a new friend, though somehow, I felt I knew him. "Yes," I said softly, and laid my head on his chest. You see, he was the tallest man I had ever seen. On my tip toes, my head only came to his shoulders.

I pondered the meaning of the dream . . .

The crowd was abused persons, mostly women. Only a few men joined us. We were all dressed alike, because we had all been through the same pain. The hospital gowns represented our healing. The exercises we were required to do was the healing process: counseling, support groups, therapy, journaling, Bible study and prayer. Pinching our dresses closed between our legs indicated we had been sexually abused. The shoes represented our progress in healing. Mine most nearly fit me but the others had on shoes far too big for them, indicating they had a long way to go. Lacing mine tighter helped me to realize I was anxious to do the best I could to make it easier on myself and at the same time, be an example for the others who were stumbling about in their awkward footwear. I must give them time and be patient.

There were some who had been observing me and were sarcastic about the process. The ones who spoke to me from behind were the abusers who mocked what I was doing and who I was doing it for. I was thrown the very large jacket of our leader, who I guessed was Jesus. The jacket was the very large task at hand. I laced the jacket carefully with prayers and study of the scriptures, each step in its place. I knew the process from the motto: "Putting the hand of the hurting in the Hand of the Healer." It looked neat and I felt satisfied with the progress.

When the jacket was given back to the leader, it became a radiant white shirt, instead. The rows and rows of pleats represented the other abuse victims and fastening the pearl buttons brought each one closer to his heart. As I helped Him with the buttoning of each of the rows, it was a mutual effort. He accepted my assistance willingly and without hesitation.

When He began to speak to me, I was fearful that my efforts had not been good enough. When He asked, "When are you going to marry me?", I was a bit confused. I thought I had already accepted the proposal, but he let me know I was doubting my efforts and methods with my question, "When are you going to ask me?" I knew I had not fully trusted before.

This time I said, "Yes" and meant it with my whole being. Never again would I doubt that I was doing less than He expected. As I laid my head on His chest, it was with peace and assurance of being accepted.

My conclusion: Do everything the very best that I can and accept the proposal!

Nature's pearls are more valuable in numbers as they are strung together. The more pearls in the grouping, the higher price it brings.

Unlike nature's pearls, pearls rescued from abuse are valuable even standing alone. They need validation that they are not the only ones. If they chance to speak out, they should be assured that their value is not diminished.

THE END

WHICH IS REALLY JUST A NEW BEGINNING!

Adult Indications Of A Hurting Childhood

Abortions
Absence of emotions
Absence of grief
Abused father/mother
Abusive opposite sex
Active/busy behavior
Addictions
Affairs during marriage
Agoraphobia (fear of open spaces)
Alcoholic parents or self
Allergy hypersensitivity
Amenorrhea/late menses
Anger
Anorexia
Anxiety
Attraction to children
Bed wetting late in childhood
Blank spaces in childhood
Bone fractures and scars
Bulimia
Childhood depression
Childhood excessive fears
Childhood grinding of teeth
Childhood masturbation
Childlike emotions in adult
Childlike voice
Choking/gagging
Claustrophobia (fear of close space)
Compulsive behaviors
Constriction of normal body
        functions
Criminal behavior
Crying uncontrollably
Dark thoughts
Dread of holidays/birthdays
Demonic presence
Denial of sexual abuse
Depression
Disgust of adult naked body as child
Distrust of authority
Drug use
Early childhood sex drive
Early puberty

Emotional black-outs
Emotional immaturity
Emotional reactions to questions
Emotionally unstable spouse
Excessive bathing
Family secrets
Fear of being alone
Fear of child being abused
Fear of dark
Fear of finding truth
Fear of gaining/losing weight
Fear of silence
Fear of snakes and spiders
Fear of trusting God
Feeling dirty
Flashbacks and intrusive thoughts
Flirting
Frequent job changes/moving
Gambling addiction
Generational abuse
God hatred
Guilt complex
Hatred of men/women
Hiding face in hair
History of marriages and divorces
Homosexuality
Impotence
Inability to forgive
Inhibition to liquid medicine
Insecurity
Insomnia
Interracial marriage
Jealousy
Lack of feelings
Lack of resistance to sexual attack
Lack of trust
Lack of friends
Lost childhood
Love of fast cars
Low self-worth
Lying/half truths
Manic depressive
Marital sexual dysfunction

Married as an escape
Masturbation
Memory gaps
Migraines
Mid-life crisis syndrome
Molesting others
Mood swings
Multiple layers of clothing
Multiple or split personality
Nail biting
Need for night light
Need for power or control
Negative thought patterns
Nightmare of snakes and spiders
Nightmares
Nudity in marriage
Obsessions
Obsessive/compulsive disorders
Occult fascination
Out-of-control emotions
Over-reactions
Overweight
Pained look in eyes
Panic attacks
Parent adoration
Phobias
Physical reactions to questions
Pleaser
PMS or PMD
Poor opposite-sex relations
Pornography in home
Post-partum depression
Powerful or fast cars
Premature physical aging
Preoccupation with personal hygiene
Preoccupation with sex
Promiscuity
Pulling out/cutting hair, eyebrows, lashes
Pyromania/impulse to set fires
Rage
Reactions to odors/smells
Refusal to nurse baby
Rejection

Remembering of bad rooms/houses
Repugnance to oral sex
Repugnance to touching by opposite sex
Repulsion when hearing scriptures or hymns
Resentments
Role reversal - parent/child
Says "I'm sorry" often
Scars (vaginal or rectal)
Secretiveness
Self-destructive behavior
Selfishness
Self-hatred
Self-mutilation
Self-protection
Self-punishment
Sexual dysfunction
Sexual relief of depression
Shyness
Sleep disorders
Social or helping work
Stress
Suicidal thoughts
Tatoos
Teen runaway
Tensions
Threatened as child
TMJ
Traumatic reaction to abuse reports
Trembling
Troubled memories
Undiagnosed pain
Uneasy with nudity in marriage
Unexplained illnesses
Unexplained vomiting
Unmet emotional needs
Unusual physical problems
Urge to molest or kill
Venereal disease in childhood
Volunteering
Withdrawal
Workaholic

Suggested Reading Resources

Books on Healing:

A Betrayal of Innocence by David Peters, [Waco, TX, Word, 1986]

Abused Boys: The Neglected Victims of Sexual Abuse by Mic Hunter [Free Press, 1989]

A Door of Hope by Jan Frank, [San Bernardino, CA, Here's Life Publications, 1987]

A Silence to be Broken by Earl D. Wilson, [Portland, OR, Multnomah Press, 1986]

Betrayal of Innocence: Incest and Its Devastation by Susan Forward and Craig Beck, [New York, NY, Penguin Books, 1979]

Beyond the Darkness by Cynthia A. Kubetin and James D. Mallory [Rapha Publishers, 1992]

Broken Boys-Mending Men by Stephen D. Grubman-Black, [Blue Ridge Summit, PA, TAB Books, 1990]

Child Sexual Abuse by Maxine Handcock and Karen Maines, [Wheaton, IL, Harold Shaw Publishing, 1987]

Cry Out by P. E. Quinn, [Abingdon Press, Nashville, 1984]

Freeing your mind from the memories that Bind by Fred and Florence Littauer [San Bernardino, CA, Here's Life Publishers, 1988]

God's Crippled Children by Lana Batemen, [8515 Greenville Avenue, Suite 103, Dallas, TX, Philippian Ministries, 1985]

Healing of Memories by David Seamands, [Wheaton, IL, Victor Books, 1985]

Males at Risk by Bolton, Morris and McEachron, [Newbury Park, CA, Sage Publications, 1989]

Never Good Enough by Carol Cannon, [Boise, ID, Pacific Press Publishing, 1993]

Pain and Pretending by Rich Buhler, [Nashville, TN, Thomas Nelson Publishers, 1988]

Secret Scars by Cynthia Crosson Tower, [New York, NY, Penguin Books, 1989]

Sins of the Father by Marianne Morris, [Boise, ID, Pacific Press Publishing, 1993]

Somewhere, A Child is Crying by Vincent J. Fontana, [New York, NY, MacMillan Publishing Company, 1973]

Stolen Childhood by Alice Husky, [Downers Grove, IL, InterVarsity Press, 1990]

Surviving the Secret by Pam Vredevelt and Kathryn Rodriguez, [Terrytown, NY, Flemming, Revell, 1992]

The Promise of Healing by Fred Littauer [Nashville, Thomas Nelson, 1992]

The Right to Innocence,by Beverly Engel, [New York, Ivy Books, 1982]

Victims No Longer by Mike Lew, [New York, NY, Nevraumont Publishing, 1985]

When Bad Things Happen to Good People Rabbi Harold S. Kushman, [New York, NY, Avon Books, 1983]

Books of Special Interest to Men:

Abused Boys: The Neglected Victims of Sexual Abuse by Mic Hunter [Free Press, 1989]

Broken Boys-Mending Men by Stephen D. Grubman-Black, [Blue Ridge Summit, PA, TAB Books, 1990]

Cry Out by P. E. Quinn, [Abingdon Press, Nashville, 1984]

Males at Risk by Bolton, Morris and McEachron, [Newbury Park, CA, Sage Publications, 1989]

Sins of the Father by Marianne Morris, [Boise, ID, Pacific Press Publishing, 1993]

The Promise of Restoration by Fred Littauer [Here's Life Publishers, San Bernadino, CA, 1990]

Victims No Longer by Mike Lew, [New York, NY, Nevraumont Publishing, 1985]

Books on Pearls:

"The Book of the Pearl: The History, Art, Science, and Industry of the Queen of Gems." by G. F. Kunz and C. H. Stevenson [Original Paper, 1993, Dover]

"The Pearl" by Fred Ward, [National Geographic, 1985]

"The Promise of the Pearl" by Leo and Bobbie Jane VanDolson (out of print)

Books on Marriage:

Communication: Key to Your Marriage by Norm Wright [Ventura, CA, Regal Books, 1979]

Growing a Great Marriage by Bob and Emilie Barnes: [Eugene, OR, Harvest House Publishers, 1988]

Intended For Pleasure by Ed and Gaye Wheat, M.D., [Old Tappan, NJ, Fleming Revell Co, 1981]

The Gift of Sex by Clifford and Joyce Penner, [Dallas, TX, Word Publishing, 1981]

The Language of Love by Gary Smalley and John Trent, Ph.D., [Denver, CO, Focus on the Family Publishers, 1988]

The Secret of Soaring by Josh McDowell, [San Bernardino, CA, Here's Life Publishers, 1985]

Devotional Books:

Facing the Brokenness (Meditations for Parents of Sexually Abused Children) by K. C. Ridding. [Herald Press, Scottsdale, PA, 1991]

Hind's Feet on High Places by Hannah Hurnard, [Wheaton, IL, Tyndale House Publishers, 1977]

My Utmost for His Highest by Oswald Chambers, [New York, Dodd, Mead and Co., 1963]

Steps to Christ by Ellen White

Books for Children

See Chapter 7.

Books on Ritual Abuse

The Occult by Josh McDowell and Don Stewart [Nashville, TN, Thomas Nelson Publishers, 1992]

Lucifer Dethroned by William and Sharon Schnoeblen [Chino, CA, Chick Publications, 1993] See also "Wicca, Satan's Little White Lie"

The Handbook for Spiritual Warfare by Dr. Ed Murphy [Nashville, TN, Thomas Nelson Publishers, 1992]

What You Need to Know About Masons by Ed Decker [Eugene, OR, Harvest House Publishers, 1992]

A Trip Into the Supernatural by Roger Morneau [Hagerstown, MD, Review & Hearald, 1982, 1993]

The Satanic Revival by Mark I Bubeck [San Bernardino, CA, Here's Life, 1991]

Halloween and Satanism by Phil Phillips and Joan Hake Robie [Lancaster, PA, Starburst Publishers, 1987] See also *Turmoil in the Toy Box.*

Masonry, Beyond the Light by William Schnoeblen [Chino, CA, Chick Publications, 1991]

This Present Darkness by Frank E. Peretti [Westchester, IL, Crossway Books, 1986]

The Fallen by Robert Don Hughes [Nashville, TN, Broadman & Holman Publishers, 1995]

Cult Watch by John Ankerberg and John Weldon [Eugene, OR, Harvest House Publishers, 1991]

Satanism, the Seduction of America's Youth by Bob Larson [Nashville, TN, Thomas Nelson Publishers, 1989]

Ritual Abuse by Margaret Smith [San Francisco, CA, Harper, 1993]

Larson's New Book of Cults by Bob Larson [Wheaton, IL, Tyndale House, 1989]